Table of

Introduction 1

How The Ketogenic Diet Works.......................... 3

Benefits Of The Ketogenic Diet......................... 8

Ketosis 11

What To Eat 18

What To Avoid......................................24

Helpful Tips & Pitfalls to Avoid..........................29

Supplements And Workouts While On Ketogenic Diet
....35

Breakfast Recipes..................................... 38

Green Smoothie Keto Breakfast 38

Scrambled Eggs w/ Guacamole Topping....................39

Breakfast Lemon Thyme Muffins 40

Bowl of Matcha Smoothie...............................42

Coconut Coffee and Ghee...............................43

Poached Egg w/ Spring Soup............................44

Brie Balls & Salted Caramel............................45

Old-Fashioned Steak and Eggs 46

Carbonara Balls 47

Low Carb & Gluten Free Breakfast Casserole ala Monte
Cristo..48

Hot Beef bacon and Avocado Balls 49

Salami & Olive Rollups 51

Egg, Beef sausage, & Cheese...........................52

Lunch Recipes..53

Tamari Marinated Steak Salad.................................53

Chicken Bites Wrapped in Garlic Beef bacon............55

Sardines Mustard Salad..56

Chicken Noodle Soup...57

Baby Zucchini Avocado Burgers..............................59

Broccoli Beef bacon Salad w/ Coconut Cream & Onions......61

Easy Sauté Zucchini Beef w/ Cilantro & Garlic.........62

Tuna Avocado Salad..63

Curried Tuna Balls..64

Chicken Skin Crisps with Aioli Egg Salad................65

Shrimp with Garlic Sauce..66

Chicken Skin Crisps Satay.......................................67

Chicken Skin Crisps Alfredo....................................69

Mediterranean Rollups...70

Smoked Salmon and Crème Fraîche Rollups............72

Dinner Recipes 73

Thai Chicken & Rice...73

Ghee Garlic Pan-Fried Cod.....................................75

Cauliflower Tabbouleh Salad...................................76

Bistek and Onions...77

Thai Chicken & Rice...78

Stir-Fried Spinach Almond.......................................80

Skewered Grilled Chicken w/ Garlic Sauce..............81

Creamy Chicken Tomato Basil Pasta.......................83

Slow Cooked Lemon Rosemary Chicken..................85

Sunflower Butter Salmon w/ Onions........................87

Chicken Skin Crisps with Spicy Avocado Cream........................88

Sweet-Savory Baked Avocado w/ Coconut & Pecans............89

Baked Avocado Crab Dynamite........................90

Spicy-Creamy Sesame Beef........................91

Thai Fish w/ Coconut & Curry........................92

Dessert Recipes........................93

Almond Butter Fudge........................93

Low Carb & Gluten-Free Bourbon Chocolate Truffles..........94

Sugar-Free, Low Carb Chocolate Mousse........................95

Rosemary Panna Cotta and Sour Cream........................97

Creamy Lemon Bars........................98

Dark Chocolate Orange Truffles........................99

Gorgonzola Panna Cotta........................101

Pumpkin Pie Mousse........................102

Herbs & Goat Cheese Panna Cotta........................103

Coconut Blueberry Cream Bars........................105

Panna Cotta Infused w/ Turmeric........................106

Low-Fat Peach Cobblers (Sugar-Free)........................107

Cheesy Prosciutto Cup Muffin........................108

Chocolate Chia Pudding........................109

Salty PB Cup Fudge........................110

Conclusion........................111

Introduction

The ketogenic diet, sometimes referred to as the "keto" diet, is a diet that includes a variety of high-fat, low-carb meals. It works similar to the Atkins diet, or other low-carb diets that people eat.

The keto diet works by significantly reducing your intake of carbohydrates and replacing them with healthy fats. By doing this, you put your body into a metabolic state that is called "ketosis". When ketosis happens, your body becomes more efficient at burning fat for energy. This is achieved by the liver turning fat into ketones which supply energy for your brain.

There are many other health benefits associated with this diet as well. Some of these other benefits of this diet include its ability to reduce blood sugar and insulin levels. All of these perks combined have been shown to have a significant amount of health benefits associated with them. We will look further into these health benefits of this diet in a few moments.

There are four different types of ketogenic diets that you can follow. For this book, we will primarily focus on the standard ketogenic diet. However, it is important to understand the other diet styles and how they may be able to benefit you. The four additional types include:

- **Standard Ketogenic Diet**: this diet consists of low carbs (5%), a moderate amount of protein (20%), and a high fat (75%) intake.

- **High-Protein Ketogenic Diet**: this variation of the diet is similar to the standard ketogenic diet, but differs in one primary aspect: it contains a higher protein content. It looks more like this: a low carb (5%), a moderate protein (35%) and a higher but still moderate fat (60%) intake.

- **Cyclical Ketogenic Diet**: this is one of the two versions of the ketogenic diet that is used by athletes and bodybuilders. This is typically the diet variation that is chosen by those who perform high cardio activities in high amounts. It follows a schedule that generally looks like this: 5 days of ketogenic diet, 2 days of high-carb intake.

- **Targeted Ketogenic Diet**: this version of the diet is also primarily used by athletes or bodybuilders, however this one is more often used by high-resistance trainers. Those who use this diet eat a standard ketogenic diet, but increase their carb intake around workouts.

Out of all four of the ketogenic diet styles, only the standard and high-protein variations have been studied extensively for their health values. The cyclical and targeted versions are more advanced and intense versions of the diet, and as stated, are primarily used by athletes and bodybuilders. They have not had any significant amount of research done to prove whether or not their more beneficial than the standard and high-protein variations, however it is believed that they do have more benefit to those who adopt higher activity levels through either cardio or high-resistance training.

How The Ketogenic Diet Works

Ketosis is the term that refers to a metabolic state in which your body is burning fat at an extremely high rate and your entire body, including your brain, runs on fat. This is because fat provides the basis for ketone bodies, where the energy molecules are found in the blood, like sugar. These energy molecules become fuel for your brain after they are converted from fat into ketones in the liver.

Your blood stream must have low levels of insulin in order to encourage ketone production. Therefore, the lower your insulin levels are, the higher your ketone levels will be. When this happens, you have reached a state that is called "optimal ketosis" which means that you are enjoying the maximum potential benefits of this low-carb diet.

When you're in the state of ketosis that is caused by the ketogenic diet, your body is deriving energy from your fat reserves instead of glucose reserves. This means that your body has constant access to energy, which translates to higher overall energy levels for you. In fact, fat has shown to have the ability to provide energy for weeks and sometimes even months at a time. Alternatively, glucose only has the ability to offer a couple of hours' worth of energy before you experience an energy crash.

Having a constant access to energy through your fat reserves can mean a few different things. First of all, you need to ensure that you are always eating the high-fat part of your diet to keep your fat reserves from running dry. This can be detrimental and destroy the entire purpose of the diet, and even cause health issues. Second, when you're in a state of optimal ketosis and you're eating a healthy diet to manage this state, you will experience a variety of positive health changes, including:

improved mental clarity and focus, increased physical endurance, and longer periods of energy with fewer energy crashes.

What Is Optimal Ketosis?

Optimal ketosis is not marked by a black and white boundary. You can't be either "in" or "out" of ketosis, as there are varying degrees of the ketosis state. Think of the measurement of ketosis as a sliding scale, and you can be anywhere from completely out of, to moderately in, to beyond optimal ketosis.

When you're testing your ketones through blood levels, you want to find yourself around 1.5-3 mmol/L to be considered at optimal ketosis. However, as long as you are above 0.5 mmol/L, you can be certain that you are experiencing at least some of the benefits of the diet. If you are below 0.5 mmol/L, you are not considered to be in ketosis at all. On the other side of the scale, anything above 3 mmol/L is unnecessary, as you have already reached peak benefits.

You never want to exceed a measurement of 8-10 mmol/L, as this is the period where you will reach ketoacidosis. If this happens, you must seek medical help immediately as this level is fatal. Please note, however, that this level is nearly impossible to reach through the ketogenic diet alone: typically, those who are experiencing these levels have underlying medical concerns and should discuss this with their doctor immediately to avoid any fatal results.

Another important thing to note is that ketoacidosis is easily achieved by those who are type 1 diabetics. Because of this factor, you should not take on this diet if you are someone who lives with type 1 diabetes. For others with existing illnesses, it is suggested that you speak with your doctor in order to make sure that this diet will be beneficial to you, and has no potential of causing any damage to your health.

Is This Diet Safe?

For the majority of people, the ketogenic diet is completely safe. In fact, for several it is even medically recommended. This diet can have the ability to reverse, manage, and prevent several illnesses and diseases that can be caused by poor dietary habits, or genetic factors. However, if you are at risk of or suffering from a disease or illness, you should always consult your doctor before making any significant dietary change, including the ketogenic diet. Having your doctor on board can help prepare you for the changes you may experience, and ensure the diet is safe and worthwhile for you.

There are some people who are not recommended to use the ketogenic diet at all. For example, if you have type 1 diabetes, are on high blood pressure medications, or are breastfeeding or pregnant, you should not eat the ketogenic diet. This diet is best suited for those who are healthy, average, or who live with the ailments that this diet is known to help with.

In order to make sure your ketones stay optimal, you will want to learn how to monitor them properly. Monitoring ketones will ensure you stay in optimal levels of ketosis, and avoid a condition called ketoacidosis. Ketoacidosis occurs when the ketones in your blood go from normal- to high-levels and your blood starts to turn acidic. This is completely unlikely for the average healthy person. However, it is important to understand what this state is, and how you should react if you ever reach it.

There are several ways to measure ketones in your blood, from urine samples, to blood samples, and even a few other ways. You can choose any method that is more comfortable for you, but the two we recommend most are the urine and blood samples. These are the easiest, most accessible, and more accurate methods for testing.

Urine samples are incredibly easy, and are likely the best choice for those with a fear of needles or blood. You simply apply urine to a test strip and it will change colors to tell you what your rating is. The colors will vary from brand to brand, but there will always be an insert to tell you further information. This is typically the first choice used by medical physicians when they are testing ketone levels.

The second best method is through blood samples. This technique is easy and the most accurate as it tests directly from the bloodstream. This test works very similar to those that are used by diabetics. First, you prick your clean finger with a loaded lancet pen, which is a tool with a little metal prick on the end that creates a small hole in your finger which will bleed a tiny bit. Then, you gently squeeze a drop of this blood on the sample strip. Once the test strip is full, the meter will register it and should give you a reading within' a few seconds.

No matter how you choose to test for ketones, it is a good idea to keep a record of each test. This record will help you in many ways. Its primary benefit is to help show you which foods and diet habits help you reach optimal ketosis. However, it can also be benefit to have on hand as you can provide this to your doctor if you ever have any health concerns.

Are There Any Side Effects?

There are a few side effects that you may encounter when you embark on the ketogenic diet journey. Aside from ketoacidosis, which we know is nearly impossible for an average person to reach through diet alone, here are some other side effects you can look out for.

These side effects are fairly normal, and occur in those who are new to the diet. Most of the effects will subside in a short period of time. Others can be avoided completely with a few simple cautionary remedies.

The Keto Flu

The infamous "keto flu" is experienced by those who are in the process of transitioning from sugar-burning to fat-burning mode. This side effect is comprised of symptoms which are similar to the actual flu, as the name suggests.

Some of these symptoms include: fatigue, nausea, headaches, cramps, and more. These symptoms can be alarming for those who are new to the diet, and may even discourage people from continuing with it. Rest assured, these are common and normal, and will subside in a short amount of time.

If you hope to avoid these symptoms altogether, there are some steps you can take to prevent your likelihood of developing them at all. The first method is to gradually reduce your carbohydrate intake, as opposed to quitting cold turkey. This can assist your body in making the transition gracefully, and minimizes the shock-factor that the sudden change could have on your body. This method is highly recommended when making any dietary changes.

An additional method, which you can use if you are currently experiencing the keto flu as well, is to drink bouillon. Drinking one to two cups daily will help increase your salt intake and minimize the effects of the keto flu. You can also try water that has been mixed with a bit of salt and lemon, if you don't prefer the taste of bouillon, or don't have any handy. The key here is to gently increase your salt intake.

Benefits Of The Ketogenic Diet

The truth of the matter is that the ketogenic diet has always been a controversial topic. Like most other treatments, health procedures, and diets, the ketogenic diet comes with its own set of drawbacks, but its health benefits most certainly exceed its drawbacks. Some of the proven health benefits of the ketogenic diet include:

Curbs Your Appetite

It is almost inevitable that if you can find a way to reduce your appetite, your battle against excess weight gain is half won. The ketogenic diet helps you curb your appetite and makes you feel less hungry because of the increased consumption of fat and proteins, which makes you feel fuller for much longer.

Increased Weight Loss

The fastest way to lose weight without starving yourself is to cut back on carbohydrates. Various studies have linked low-carb diets to increased fat loss because they help reduce insulin levels in your body, which subsequently helps eliminate excess sodium through the kidney. Eventually, this leads to excess water loss and rapid weight loss.

Helps with Abdominal Fat Loss

If you've been struggling with weight loss for a while, you probably realize that abdominal fat is the most difficult type of fat to get rid of. Sometimes, people tend to lose weight in other parts of their body but are still unable to lose the fat in their stomach. This is because the type of fat that is stored in your abdomen is visceral fat, which is a very stubborn kind of fat. The good news is that low carbohydrate diets like the ketogenic diet are very effective at getting rid of abdominal fat.

Reduces Triglycerides

Triglycerides are fat molecules in your body that are known to increase the risk for heart diseases. Low-carb diets such as the ketogenic diet are able to reduce triglycerides in the blood and prevent heart diseases caused by excessive triglycerides in the body.

Increased HDL Levels

High Density Lipoprotein, also known as HDL, is a type of lipoprotein that helps to carry cholesterol around the body. Some people love to refer to it as 'the good cholesterol' because of its health benefits as compared to the Low Density Lipoprotein, LDL, known as 'the bad cholesterol'. Increased HDL levels in your body helps ensure that cholesterol is eliminated from the body by transporting it to the liver for reuse or excretion. This is unlike the LDL, which carries the cholesterol from the liver back into the body. Consuming a lot of healthy fats, as is observed in the ketogenic diet, helps to increase HDL levels in the body.

Reduces Blood Sugar Levels

People who suffer from Type 2 diabetes can also benefit from the ketogenic diet as it helps to lower blood sugar and insulin levels in the body. When you consume carbohydrates, your body breaks it down into glucose in your digestive tract, and then sends it into your bloodstream as glucose, which consequently increases your blood sugar levels. This increase in blood sugar levels is very harmful to your body, so your body tries to protect itself by producing insulin hormones to burn or store the excess glucose. People who do not have any insulin resistance problems are able to get their blood glucose levels reduced really quickly. However, the cells of those who suffer from insulin resistance have a hard responding to insulin. This makes it difficult for the body to balance your blood glucose levels, and this eventually leads to what is known as type 2 diabetes. The good news is that a low-carbohydrate diet can help your body eliminate excess blood glucose without the help of insulin.

Helps in Treating Metabolic Syndrome

Metabolic syndrome is a serious condition that is associated with increased blood pressure, high blood sugar levels, excess body fat and abdominal fat, and high triglycerides. These conditions can increase your risk of developing diabetes, stroke, and other heart-related diseases. The ketogenic diet can significantly help counter and prevent metabolic syndrome.

The truth is; you cannot derive all these benefits if you don't get into a state of optimal ketosis.

Ketosis

In the human body, there are three main storage 'depots' of fuel that can be tapped into for energy when there is a caloric deficiency.

*Protein storage, which is converted into glucose in your liver

*Carbohydrate (glycogen) storage

*Fat storage, Your body can also utilize its fat storage for energy, which is stored as body fat.

There is a fourth type of fuel that your body can use for energy as well. It is known as ketones. On a normal day, ketones are insignificant to the body when it comes to energy production. However, on a low-carbohydrate diet, such as the Ketogenic diet, ketones are used a lot as a source of energy, especially by the brain.

Body tissues always make use of the most available source of fuel in the bloodstream. For instance, if there is a high concentration of glucose in the body, the body chooses glucose as its most preferred source of fuel, with the exception of a few organs like the heart, which uses a mixture of glucose, ketones, and free fatty acids for fuel.

If however, there is a reduction in glucose levels in your body, the next available source of fuel takes precedence as the main source of energy. On a ketogenic diet, the body switches from using glucose as its primary source of fuel, to utilizing stored fats, which are readily available. One of the goals of the ketogenic diet is to increase the concentration of proteins and fats in the body while getting rid of carbohydrates, in order to facilitate the usage of excess fat stored in the body for energy.

Other factors that influence which fuels your body uses for energy include levels of insulin and glucagon hormones, as well as concentrations of regulatory enzymes for breaking down glucose and fats.

Ketone Bodies and Ketogenesis

There are three known types of ketone bodies, namely Acetoacetate, Beta-hydroxybutyrate and Acetone. The process by which these ketones are formed is what is known as ketogenesis. In order to understand ketosis properly, it is important to fully grasp the concept of ketogenesis. Ketogenesis in your body depends on two major factors; the liver and fat cells.

Fat Cells

The breakdown of fat cells in the body depends on the catecholamine and the insulin hormones. When there are high levels of insulin in your blood, it prevents the mobilization of free fatty acids and increases fat storage in the body through something called a lipoprotein lipase enzyme (LPL).

As the insulin levels in the blood go down, the mobilization of FFAs goes up. The FFAs are flow into the bloodstream where they bind with a protein known as Albumin, and are then used for energy production. FFAs that are not used for fuel get oxidized in the liver. This oxidation leads to the production of ketone bodies, which are then released back into the bloodstream.

Liver

The liver also plays a major role in ketogenesis. Ketones are produced in the liver, even if you are on a ketogenic diet, but in small and insignificant quantities, and the amount of available glycogen in your body determines whether or not your liver can produce ketone bodies.

The main function of glycogen in the liver is to help maintain normal blood glucose levels. So when you are on a low-carb diet, and your blood glucose levels are reduced, the liver glycogen prompts the liver to break down its glycogen stores and release glucose into the bloodstream. Your body makes use of this glucose for some time (between 12 and 16 hours depending on your level of physical activity), after your glycogen stores become depleted. Upon depletion, ketogenesis increases rapidly utilizing the available FFAs.

Metabolic Effects of The Ketogenic Diet

One topic that always raises controversy whenever the ketogenic diet comes under the spotlight is whether the diet can mess up your metabolism.

Basically, the main purpose of your metabolic system is to make fuels available in your body whenever they are needed. As you continue on with the diet, your metabolic system continues to work to ensure that the energy from the foods you eat is appropriately allocated and the excess stored. The average human today eats much more than is recommended, and as a result the metabolic system has to cope with more work than it is designed to handle. During the starvation diet, your metabolic system concentrates on providing glucose to tissues that need it to function, for instance, the brain, kidney, red blood cells, etc.

This glucose is usually obtained from your body's protein stores; mainly the muscles and sometimes fat. As your body continues to utilize proteins from the muscles for energy, your muscle mass begins to go decrease, leaving your metabolic system with two challenges; how to continue supplying glucose to the glucose-dependent tissues, and how to maintain muscle mass so that your body doesn't become too weak to function.

Your metabolic system doesn't know how long this starvation will last, it could be a few hours or a couple of weeks. It first tries to cope by plundering the glucose supply in your blood, before proceeding to the proteins in your muscles. But because it must also ensure that your muscle mass is not excessively depleted, it is forced to turn to the ketones for energy.

Ketones stand in for glucose and proteins, sparing your muscles from being depleted. This is what happens on a starvation diet.

On a typical low-carb diet, you would need to consume some proteins and fats in order to preserve your muscles. The proteins you consume are converted to glucose. The question is, will a low-carb diet ruin your metabolism?

Your metabolism is not just dependent on what you eat, but on a number of other factors, including your basal metabolic rate (BMR), thermic effect of food (TEF) and physical activity.

Basal Metabolic Rate

Your BMR is dependent on the amount of lean body mass you have, your hormonal homeostasis, hereditary tendencies, and your present body fat levels, amongst other factors.

Going on a diet affects your basal metabolic rate and hormone production by interfering with your body composition.

Thermic Effect of Food

The macronutrients from the foods you eat are broken down and processed into energy, most of which get accounted for by protein. This is the reason why low carb diets improve your metabolism through an increased consumption of protein - typically, when you eat protein, you burn 30% of those calories just digesting the food - which is why eating protein helps with weight loss.

Thermic Effect of Activity

This refers to any form of activity that is not a typical body movement, such as exercise. People who are physically inactive and lead sedentary lifestyles generally only burn 10-30% more calories above their BMR. Physically active people, on the other hand, tend to burn more. This basically means that your metabolism is affected by much more than the food you eat, as long as you maintain a moderate level of physical activity and avoid complete starvation you can maintain a healthy metabolism.

How to Enter Ketosis

In order to be successful with the ketogenic diet, you need to adhere to a number of principles:

*__Eat More Fat__: 60-75% of your daily calories should come from fat, 15-30% from protein and only 5-10% should come from carbohydrates.

*__Eat Less Than 50 grams of Carbs__: Your daily net carbs consumption should be less than 50 grams. Daily net carbs are calculated by deducting fiber contents from carbohydrate contents.

*__Eat Moderate Protein__: Eat moderate amounts of proteins. You can use your body fat percentage to determine your ideal protein intake per day. Generally, you should take between 0.6 and 1 gram per pound of lean body mass.

*__Eat Healthy Fats__: Let most of your fat calories come from the healthy kinds alternatives, particularly monounsaturated fats, saturated fats and omega 3s.

*__Avoid Fruits__: If your net carb limit is low, you should avoid fruits and other low-carb treats.

*__Eat When Hungry__: Don't starve yourself. Ensure that you eat whenever you are hungry.

*Drink Lots of Water: While it helps to keep an eye on your calorie intake, you should never ignore your body's needs. Drink at least 2-3 liters of water daily.

*Stock Up: Stock up on healthy foods like non-starchy vegetables, meat, eggs, coconut oil, avocado, macadamia nuts, bone broth and other fermented foods, saturated fats, and unsaturated fats.

*Avoid Garbage Fats: Avoid processed fats like vegetable oils, fully and partially hydrogenated oils, margarine, trans fats, soybean oil, corn oil and canola oil.

*Raw, Organic, Local: Raw and organic dairy products are also good as long as you don't have any allergies. However, you should try to avoid milk due to its high carb content or opt for unpasteurized full-fat milk if you have to.

*More Electrolytes: Increase your electrolyte intake. The ketogenic diet may cause sodium, calcium and potassium deficiencies, so you should increase your intake of mushrooms, salmon and avocados for potassium; nuts or magnesium supplements for magnesium; and salt or bone broth for sodium.

*Less Processed Foods: Avoid processed foods as these tend to contain hidden carbs such as sorbitol, maltitol, preservatives, additives and artificial sweeteners. To be on the safe side, be sure to always read the labels when shopping.

*Skip "Fat Free": Ignore any foods labeled low-fat, fat-free, or low-carb, as these usually contain extra carbs and artificial additives.

*Avoid Sweets: If you are using any medications that contain sugars or sweeteners, ask for the sugar-free variety. Make sure you always plan your diet in advance to avoid temptation and spontaneous eating.

*Plan Your Meals and Shopping: Shop weekly and get rid of anything that is not allowed on the diet from your home. Have salads and hard boiled eggs available in case you feel like snacking.

Let us now get to the specifics; what should you eat and what should you avoid while on a ketogenic diet in order to get into a state of ketosis effortlessly? Let's start with what to eat.

What To Eat

While on the ketogenic diet, it's important to know what to eat and what to avoid. Let's start with what to eat.

<u>Veggies</u>:

The ketogenic diet recommends consuming a variety of veggies, including kale, cucumber, broccoli, asparagus, collard greens and mushrooms. Vegetables are a great source of vitamins which enhance your immune system against diseases, especially the leafy green veggies. Though some vegetables are high in sugar, you can go for organic vegetables that have better nutritional value.

Veggies allowed in ketogenic diets should be high in nutrients and low on carbohydrates. They are usually dark and leafy such as spinach and kale. Other veggies you can include in your diet are: onions, tomatoes, and garlic. Here is a full list:

*Onion
*Garlic
*Artichoke hearts
*Broccoli
*bib lettuce
*Arugula
*Romaine
*Cauliflower
*Brussel sprouts
*Cabbage
*Cucumbers
*Mushrooms
*Asparagus
*Peppers such as banana, bell and jalapeno
*Squashes such as butternut and spaghetti Proteins

Proteins:

There are several reasons why proteins play a major role in ketosis. First, protein intake is beneficial to your body because it facilitates general growth and repair of worn out cells. Proteins also help in the synthesis and monitoring of certain hormones in your blood stream that regulate various bodily functions.

In a ketogenic diet plan, your protein intake should be just enough to satisfy your daily protein requirements. This is because an excessive intake of proteins may cause your body to resort to breaking down the proteins into energy. In such a case, the body will disintegrate its own tissues and wear itself out in the process. There are various sources of protein in the ketogenic diet, which include:

Seafood, either canned or fresh:

*Oysters
*Sardines
*Salmon
*Albacore
*Tuna
*Crab
*Scallops
*Cod
*Tilapia
*Lobster
*Shrimp

Dairy Products:

Here, you need to avoid regular cow's milk, which is usually rich in sugar, and go for heavy creams instead. You can eat these dairy products:

*Full-fat cream cheese

*Butter, but you should avoid margarine

*Full-fat sour cream

*Heavy whipping cream

*Full-fat cheeses

Meat Products:

The key is to get meat products that are rich in fat to supplement the high fat requirement in the ketogenic diet. However, you can eat lean meat if you can add oils such as organic olive and coconut oils. Here are some meats to choose from:

*Sausages

*Steak

*Eggs

*Ground beef

*Cured Meats, especially pepperoni, salami, prosciutto

*Deli meats, but be careful to avoid those with added ingredients or fillers

*Bacon

*Chicken, aim for skin-on breasts, and thighs, wings, and drumsticks

*Roasts (Beef/ Lamb) or Ribs (Beef/ Lamb)

Fats and Oils:

Fats are grouped into various categories, depending on their health benefits to the body. The most recommended fats are omega 3 fatty oils, including salmon, tuna, and trout. Saturated and monounsaturated fats such as butter, macadamia nuts, avocados, egg yolks and coconut oil are also great for weight loss through ketosis. They are preferred because they have a stable chemical structure which is less inflammatory. The following types of food can be a great source of fat and oil in your ketogenic diet plan:

*Chicken fat
*Peanut butter
*Avocado Butter
*Coconut oil
*Olive oil
*Non hydrogenated lard
*MCT Oil
*Macadamia Nut Oil
*Avocado Oil
*Red Palm Oil
*Ghee
*Butter
*Olive oil
*Duck fat
*Beef tallow

On the other hand, you need to reduce your intake of omega 6 fatty acids and trans-fats, the latter of which are hydrogenated fats that are bad for your health. If you are the kind of person who likes to fry everything, go for non-hydrogenated options such as ghee and coconut oil. This will ensure minimum oxidation of these oils, and provide you with the essential oils. The inflammatory omega 6 fatty oils are usually derived from nut or seed based foods.

Spices, Drinks, And Sweeteners:

The ketogenic diet offers a variety of food flavors that allow you to sharpen your kitchen skills with spices and natural sweeteners. You are free to experiment with pure ground spices such as cinnamon, turmeric, black pepper, parsley, chili powder, garlic, and rosemary. However, you need to be careful when choosing spices as some may contain added sugars such as powdered dextrose. When it comes to beverages, stick to only those that do not contain added sugars, or better yet use sweeteners such as stevia and monk fruit to satisfy your sweet tooth. Here are some condiments you can use:

*Lemon/Lime Juice

*Salad dressings, acceptable ones are full-fat Ranch, Caesar, Bleu Cheese and Italian

*Hot sauce

*Soy sauce as a gluten-free option

*Mustard Mayonnaise

Fruit:

You can incorporate fruit, but in moderation, since some fruits tend to contain carbs that trigger weight gain. You can eat these fruits:

*Cranberries

*Strawberries

*Blackberries

*Raspberries

*Blueberries

* Avocado

Nuts & Seeds:

Just like with fruits, you need to regulate the amount of nuts and seeds you eat in order to minimize carb consumptions. These nuts are recommended for you:

*Flax seeds

*Pumpkin seeds

*Sunflowers seeds

*Sesame seeds

*Pecans

*Walnuts

*Pistachios

*Macadamias

*Hazelnuts

*Almonds

Let's now get into what to avoid while on a ketogenic diet.

What To Avoid

The ketogenic diet doesn't allow high carb or sugary foods, grains and related products, corn, tubers, legumes and milk.

Milk

While milk is rich in protein and fat, it is also loaded with sugar in the form of lactose, especially skim milk. However, fermented milk products have less lactose since the bacteria used in fermentation tends to consume all the lactose. This means that you can enjoy a few glasses of yoghurt with no problems.

Sugars:

Avoid most sweet products, or any food substance that contains brown sugar, cane sugar, corn syrup, honey or sucrose. The majority of packaged or processed foods are high in wheat and sugars and have high concentrations of carbohydrates. You should also avoid canned soups and stews, as most of these contain hidden starchy thickeners.

Avoid these sugary foods and processed products in general:

*Coconut sugar, date sugar
*Sorghum, molasses
*Fructose, crystalline fructose
*Fruit syrup, fruit juice concentrates
*Tapioca syrup
*Glucose, lactose, glycerol and dextrose
*Maltose, barley malt, and malt powder
*Honey, agave nectar, brown rice syrup, invert sugar syrup
*Cane sugar, cane juice, cane juice crystals, cane syrup
*Brown sugar
*Canned soups and stews
*Syrups, such as golden syrup, malt syrup, maple syrup and rice syrup

In addition, avoid snacks that are processed or that contain added sugars, for instance:

*Chips
*Wheat Thins
*Sun Chips
*Pretzels
*Triscuits
*Cookies
*Pastries

Grains:

Avoid both grains and products made from grains due to their high carb content. Most wheat products are also rich in sugars and should be avoided, including:

*Pretzels
*Cakes, pies
*Cookies, tarts
*Crackers
*Tortillas
*Cold cereals, hot cereals
*Pasta
*Waffles, pancakes
*Cereals
*English muffins
*Sandwiches
*Wheat Thins
*Oatmeal
*Corn
*High-fructose corn syrup
*Pancakes
*Breads, muffins, rolls, bread crumbs

Sugary Beverages:

These comprise of drinks like fruit and vegetable juices, non-diet sodas, and alcohol. Juices are generally prepared from the concentrated sugars of the original fruit, while non-diet sodas such as corn syrup contain large amounts of fructose. Alcohol, on the other hand, is a product of grain, which has a high carb-content. If you have to drink, go for low carb beers.

Generally, you should avoid:

*Non-diet sodas
*Sweet or dessert wines
*Juice from fruits
*Beers
*Whiskey
*Rum
*Alcohol and mixers
*Tequila
*Vodka

You should also steer away from energy drinks, as these usually have high sugar content. This means that you should ditch the following brands:

*Monster
*Red bull
*Starbucks refreshers
*Mountain Dew MDX
*XS Energy Drinks
*5 hour Energy

Corn:

Avoid corn and corn products such as cornbread, corn chips, popcorn, and cornmeal. Corn can be used as a thickener or preservative in other products; therefore, remember to read the label.

Avoid:

*Cornmeal
*Popcorn
*Polenta
*Grits
*Corn chips
*Tamale wrappers
*Cornbread

Starchy Tubers

Avoid potatoes, sweet potatoes, and yams, as well as related products such as potato chips, french fries, and taters.

Starchy veggies
*Artichokes
*Okra
*Peas
*Lima beans
*Sweet potatoes
*Corn
*Acorn squash
*Beets
*Potatoes
*Yucca
*Butternut squash
*Yam

Legumes

Though legumes are said to contain proteins, you should avoid them due to their high starch content. Excellent examples include beans, peanuts, and lentils. Other beans that you shouldn't eat include:

*Navy beans
*Red beans
*String beans
*Pinto beans
*Green beans
*White beans
*Broad beans
*Garbanzo beans
*Kidney beans
*Mung beans
*Black beans
*Fava beans
*Horse beans
*Lima beans
*Adzuki beans

Peas

*Chickpeas
*Sugar snap peas
*Black-eyed peas
*Snow peas

Other Legumes

*Peanuts
*Miso
*Lupins
*Soybeans
*Tofu
*Peanut butter
*Lentils
*Mesquite
*All soybean products and derivatives

Helpful Tips & Pitfalls to Avoid

When you fast, the hormones in your body will change. The keto plan is similar to this process. You could achieve ketosis in just a couple of days once you have used up all of your stored glycogen. It can take a month, a week, or just a few days. It all depends on which type of method you choose. Your protein and carbohydrate intake will determine the time. Exercise also plays a vital role.

How to Know When You Are in Ketosis

Whether you have taken any tests to discover your ketosis status, your body will exhibit physical signs to prompt you. You may have a loss of appetite, increased thirst, have bad breath, or notice a stronger urine smell. These are all clues from your body. This is how it all happens:

Bad Breath Flares: You may notice a metallic or fruity taste with an odor similar to nail polish remover. This is the by-product of acetoacetic acid (acetone) which is an obvious indication of ketosis. You may also experience a drier mouth. These changes are normal as a side effect as your body processes high-fat foods.

Once you are accustomed to the ketogenic dieting techniques, the bad breath symptoms will pass. If you are socializing, try a diet soda or a non-sugary drink. Sugar-free gum is also a quick fix. Always check the nutrition labels for carbohydrate facts; you may be surprised. Diet soda and gum is not generally allowed on the keto diet because they reduce ketones. Therefore, only use it temporarily. If you are at home, just grab the toothbrush.

<u>Thirst is Increased</u>: Fluid retention is increased when you are consuming carbohydrates. Once the carbs are flushed away, water weight is lost. You counter-balance by increasing your water intake since you are probably dehydrated.

The ketogenic diet requires more water since as a result, you are storing carbs. If you are dehydrated; your body can use the stored carbs to restore hydration. When you're in ketosis, the carbs are removed, and your body doesn't have the water reserves. If you have tried other diets, you might have been dehydrated, but the higher carbohydrate counts stopped you from being thirsty. Thus, the keto state is a diuretic state, so drink plenty of water daily.

<u>Ketosis and Your Sleep Patterns</u>: After you have a good night of sleep, your body is in ketosis since you have fasted for over eight hours, you are on the way to burning ketones. If you are new to the high-fat and low-carb dieting, the optimal fat-burning state takes time. Your body has depended on bringing in carbs and glucose; it will not readily give up carbs and start to crave saturated fats.

A restless night is also a normal side effect. Vitamin supplements can sometimes remedy the problem that can be caused by a lowered insulin and serotonin level. For a quick fix; try one-half of a tablespoon of fruit spread and a square of chocolate. It sounds crazy, but it works! However, you still need to count the carbs of your medicine.

<u>Lowered Appetite</u>: When you reduce your carbs and proteins, you will be increasing your fat intake. The reduced appetite comes from the multitude of fibrous veggies, fats, and satiating nutrients provided in the new diet. The 'full-factor' is a huge benefit to the ketogenic plan. It will give you one less thing to worry about – being hungry.

Pungent Urine Smells: With the high acetone levels, your urine is also a strong clue to ketosis (its darkened color). There is no reason for concern; it's just your body adjusting to the new status.

Digestive Issues: You have made a huge change in your diet overnight. It's expected you may have problems including constipation or diarrhea when you first start the keto diet. That's why you must drink plenty of water, or you could easily become constipated because of dehydration. The low-carbs contribute to the issue.

Each person is different, and it will depend on what foods you have chosen to eat to increase your fiber intake. You may experience issues because your fiber intake may be too high in comparison to your previous diet. Try reducing new foods until the transitional phase of ketosis is concluded. It should clear up with time.

You may be lacking beneficial bacteria. Try consuming fermented foods to increase your probiotics and aid digestion. You can benefit from B vitamins, omega 3 fatty acids, and beneficial enzymes as well. Eat the right veggies and add a small amount of salt to your food to help with the movements. If all else fails, try some Milk of Magnesia.

Other Possible Physical Side Effects

Induction Flu: The diet can make you irritable, nauseous, a bit confused, lethargic, and possibly suffer from a lingering headache. Several days into the plan should remedy these effects. If not, add one-half of a teaspoon of salt to a glass of water, and drink it to help with the side effects. You may need to do this once a day for about the first week, and it could take about 15 to 20 minutes before it helps. It will go away!

Heart Palpitations: You may begin to feel 'fluttery' as a result of dehydration or because of an insufficient intake of salt. Try to make adjustments, but if you don't feel better quickly, you should seek emergency care.

Leg Cramps: The loss of magnesium (a mineral) can be a demon and create a bit of pain with the onset of the keto diet plan changes. With the loss of the minerals during urination, you could experience attacks of cramps in your legs.

Helpful Tips

Only Eat When You're Hungry: One outstanding benefit of the keto diet plan is that you don't stay hungry. This is a common mistake when people first start a new diet, but with the ketogenic method, you can have the fats. Carbs and fats are your two major sources of energy for your body. If you are removing the carbs, they must be replaced by fats. Remove both elements, and you would starve. By consuming natural fats, you are satisfied. Enjoy eggs, fatty fish, coconut and olive oil, bacon, meat, butter, and full-fat cream.

When your body doesn't have insulin that stores the fat, you will become a fat-burning machine and start dropping those unwanted pounds. Trust your instincts and cut out one of the meals or eat several times a day but keep track of the carbs.

The Stalling and Plateaus of Weight Loss

At first, you may not notice the weight loss. There could be days or weeks where you don't notice the changes, but slow is the best method. You are altering your lifestyle and breaking old habits. You need to remain patient because there aren't any quick fixes to weight loss.

As with any new challenge, the initial phase of a long-term challenge is difficult. Once you have discovered how easy the ketogenic plan is; you will wonder how it took you so long to try it.

Check Your Medications

It's important to inform your doctor of your weight loss program. He/she may prescribe some medicines that make you gain weight. These are a few to question:

Insulin Injections: If taken in high doses, your insulin can impede weight loss. By consuming fewer carbs, you are essentially reducing the requirement of insulin. Again, ask your healthcare professional before you make any changes.

Other Possible Medications Causing Weight Gain:

- Oral contraceptives
- Antidepressants
- Epilepsy drugs
- Blood pressure medications
- Allergy medicines
- Antibiotics

More Sleep & Less Stress

If you are a victim of sleep deprivation, you will understand how stressful everyday life is, even before you begin a diet plan. You may believe it's too late for you, but it isn't. Your diet plan will work, but you may need to make a few other adjustments.

Chronic stress will increase your cortisol levels – the stress hormone. With that action, your hunger levels also increase. The result is that you eat more and put on the weight. It's important to find ways to remove the stress; whether it is decluttering your home or taking a vacation.

Eliminate coffee or other forms of caffeine early in the afternoon and don't consume alcohol for at least three hours before bedtime. Alcohol will also interfere with your quality of sleep which is why you wake up feeling tired after an evening of nightclubs and boozing.

If you enjoy working out for your health, be sure to do that at least four hours before time for sleeping. Make sure your room is sufficient darkness. You will wake refreshed, ready to face your tasty ketogenic breakfast.

Supplements And Workouts While On Ketogenic Diet

Why Supplement?

On any diet, supplementation is not a necessity, but beneficial. The same can be said for a ketogenic diet.

The reason for supplementing is often in order to maximise your intake of a certain macro/micronutrient if the diet requires you to eat a large quantity of it, or if it restricts certain foods, like carbohydrates, meaning you miss out on some key nutrients.

#1 Omega 3

Omega 3 is an essential fatty acid which is found from dietary sources of oily fish such as mackerel, salmon and sardines. It cannot be synthesised in the body; therefore, it must be taken in through our diets.

For many people, it is not possible to eat fish in such highquantities in order to receive the optimal levels of omega 3, as well as omega 6 and 9. Therefore, supplementing with omega 3 supplements such as fish oil is a great way to boost your intake.

There has also been research to suggest that fish oil supplements can lower levels of blood triglycerides. This is especially beneficial whilst on a ketogenic diet, since one of the risks when following it is that your levels of blood triglycerides may become too high.

By supplementing with omega 3 and fish oil supplements, you can help combat this and enjoy the benefits of the ketogenic diet, without worrying about any side effects.

#2 Coconut Oil

Coconut oil is an excellent 'supplement' which can be utilised for many different health benefits. It is excellent for the ketogenic diet, since it can be used in order to boost your fat intake. What's more, its excellent for boosting your healthy fat intake.

Coconut oil is one of the only plant based fat sources which is saturated. This means if you want to get enough saturated fat in your diet, but do not want to have unhealthy, heavily processed fats, or animal fats, then coconut oil is a must.

You can purchase coconut oil in its raw form, which can be used for cooking, oil pulling, among others, or in the form of capsules, which might be more easy to take for someone who is just looking to increase their intake of healthy fats.

#3 Whey Protein

Possibly the most widely known and popular supplement out there. Whey protein is the most bio-available protein, and isquickly digested.

The reason you would take a whey protein supplement would be if you cannot get enough protein into your diet due to either cost, or because you need to minimise intake of other macronutrients.

Whilst on the ketogenic diet, since you are restricting where you get your calories from, it is a good idea to take protein supplements to ensure that you do not have to worry about consuming any carbs, or even fat from protein sources, meaning you have more room to play with elsewhere.

#4 Spirulina

Supplementing with greens such as spirulina is an excellent way of boosting the amount of vitamins and minerals you intake when following a ketogenic diet. spirulina-powder

What's more, spirulina is what is known as a complete protein, meaning that it contains all of the amino acids which your body needs in order to function properly.

Furthermore, spirulina contains moderate amounts of fibre. This makes it brilliant when following a ketogenic diet, since fibre helps to bind with carbohydrates and prevent them from being stored as fat.

#5 BCAAs

BCAAs, or branched chain amino acids, are a great supplement for all sorts of different individuals when following different diets.

One of the main benefits of BCAAs is to prevent muscle loss, especially when you are following a catabolic (tissue breakdown) meal plan. A ketogenic diet is just this, catabolic, since you are breaking down fat in order to lose weight. The issue is that you will lose some muscle. By supplementing with BCAAs, you can prevent your body from breaking down as much muscle as it normally would.

Furthermore, they can reduce the time it takes for your body to recover, which is vital when in a caloric deficit.

Breakfast Recipes

Green Smoothie Keto Breakfast

Prep time: 5 min; Cook time: 0 min

Serving Size: 1 glass; **Serves**: 1

Calories: 380; **Total Fat**: 30 g; **Protein**: 12 g;

Total Carbs: 13 g; **Net Carbs**: 5 g; **Sugar**: 0 g; **Fiber**: 8 g;

Ingredients

- 10 pcs. of raw almonds
- 2 cups of kale or spinach
- 2 pcs. of Brazil nuts
- 1 scoop of Amazing Grass Greens Powder or green powder of your choice
- 1 cup of unsweetened coconut milk (from a refrigerated carton and not in can)

Instructions

1. Place the almonds, spinach, coconut milk and Brazil nuts into the blender.
2. Blend the ingredients until pureed.
3. Add the rest of the ingredients.
4. Blend well.
5. Serve in a tall glass and enjoy.

Scrambled Eggs w/ Guacamole Topping

Prep time: 5 min; Cook time: 10 min

Serving Size: 1 plate; **Serves**: 1

Calories: 442; **Total Fat**: 23 g; **Protein**: 18 g;

Total Carbs: 4 g; **Net Carbs**: 2 g; **Sugar**: 0 g; **Fiber**: 2 g;

Ingredients

- 3 medium-sized eggs
- 1 Tbsp. of coconut oil
- ¼ cup of guacamole (any brand like Wholly Guacamole)
- 1 pinch of salt, to taste

Instructions

1. Put coconut oil in the pan.
2. Put the eggs, and scramble over low heat setting.
3. Transfer the scrambled eggs into a serving plate.
4. Top eggs with guacamole.
5. Add a pinch of salt, if desired.
6. Serve and enjoy.

Breakfast Lemon Thyme Muffins

Prep time: 15 min; **Cook time**: 20 min

Serving Size: 2 muffins; **Serves**: 6

Calories: 300; **Total Fat**: 28 g; **Protein**: 11 g;

Total Carbs: 7 g; **Net Carbs**: 4 g; **Sugar**: 1 g; **Fiber**: 3 g;

Ingredients

- 3 cups of almond flour
- 4 medium-sized eggs
- 2 tsp. of lemon thyme
- ½ cup of melted ghee
- 1 tsp. of baking soda
- ½ tsp. of salt, to taste

Equipment needed

- Muffin pan
- Muffin liners

Instructions

1. Pre-heat oven to 350° F.
2. Put ghee in mixing bowl and melt.
3. Add baking soda and almond flour.
4. Put the eggs in.
5. Add the lemon thyme (if preferred, other herbs or spices may be used).
6. Drizzle with salt.
7. Mix all ingredients well.
8. Line the muffin pan with liners.
9. Spoon mixture into the pan, filling the pan to about ¾ full.
10. Bake for about 20 minutes. Test by inserting a toothpick into a muffin. If it comes out clean, then the muffins are done.
11. Serve immediately.

Bowl of Matcha Smoothie

Prep time: 10 min; Cook time: 0 min

Serving Size: 1 bowl; **Serves**: 1

Calories: 420; **Total Fat**: 28 g; **Protein**: 13 g;

Total Carbs: 25 g; **Net Carbs**: 8 g; **Sugar**: 6 g; **Fiber**: 17 g;

Ingredients

- 1 tsp. of matcha powder
- 1 scoop of greens powder (if desired)
- 8 oz. of coconut yogurt (may be substituted w/ regular Greek yogurt if you have no problems with dairy)
- 1 Tbsp. of goji berries
- 1 Tbsp. of chia seeds
- 1 Tbsp. of cacao nibs
- 1 Tbsp. of coconut flakes
- Stevia, to taste

Instructions

1. Blend the yogurt with the matcha powder. Sweeten with stevia, if preferred.
2. Transfer the smoothie into a regular-sized bowl.
3. Top the smoothie with goji berries, chia seeds, cacao nibs, and coconut flakes
4. Serve and enjoy.

Coconut Coffee and Ghee

Prep time: 5 - 10 min; **Cook time**: 0 min

Serving Size: 1 cup; **Serves**: 1

Calories: 150; **Total Fat**: 15 g; **Protein**: 0 g;

Total Carbs: 0 g; **Net Carbs**: 0 g; **Sugar**: 0 g; **Fiber**: 0 g;

Ingredients

- ½ Tbsp. of coconut oil
- ½ Tbsp. of ghee
- 1 to 2 cups of preferred coffee (or rooibos or black tea, if preferred)
- 1 Tbsp. of coconut or almond milk

Instructions

1. Place the almond (or coconut) milk, coconut oil, ghee and coffee in a blender (or milk frother).
2. Process for around 10 seconds or until the coffee turns creamy and foamy.
3. Pour contents into a coffee cup.
4. Serve immediately and enjoy.

Poached Egg w/ Spring Soup

Prep time: 10 min; **Cook time**: 20 min

Serving Size: 1 bowl; **Serves**: 2

Calories: 150; **Total Fat**: 5 g; **Protein**: 16 g;

Total Carbs: 11 g; **Net Carbs**: 4 g; **Sugar**: 5 g; **Fiber**: 7 g;

Ingredients

- **32 oz. of chicken broth**
- 2 regular-sized eggs
- 1 head romaine lettuce, chopped
- 1 pinch of salt, to taste

Instructions

1. Boil the chicken broth.
2. Turn the heat down, then poach the eggs in the broth for around 5 minutes or until slightly runny.
3. Get the eggs and transfer into separate bowls.
4. Place the chopped romaine lettuce in the soup, and cook for 3 to 5 minutes or until wilted slightly.
5. Using a ladle, transfer the broth into the 2 bowls.
6. Serve while hot and enjoy immediately.

Brie Balls & Salted Caramel

Prep time: 5 min; Cook time: 0 min

Serving Size: 1 ball; **Serves**: 6

Calories: 130; **Total Fat**: 12 g; **Protein**: 5 g;

Total Carbs: 1 g; **Net Carbs**: 0 g; **Sugar**: 1 g; **Fiber**: 1 g;

Ingredients

- 4 oz. of Brie cheese, chopped roughly
- 2 oz. of salted macadamia nuts
- ½ tsp. of caramel flavor

Instructions

1. Place all ingredients in a small-sized food processor and pulse until a coarse dough is formed or around half a minute.
2. Using a spoon, form 6 balls from the mixture.
3. Serve and enjoy immediately. If desired, refrigerate for no more than 3 days before consuming.

Old-Fashioned Steak and Eggs

Prep time: 15 min; **Cook time**: 30 min

Serving Size: 1 plate; **Serves**: 1

Calories: 687; **Total Fat**: 52 g; **Protein**: 43 g;

Total Carbs: 5 g; **Net Carbs**: 5 g; **Sugar**: 0 g; **Fiber**: 0 g;

Ingredients:

- 4 oz. of sirloin steak (or any preferred steak cut)
- 3 large-sized eggs
- 1 Tbsp. of butter
- 1 Tbsp. of olive oil
- ½ avocado
- Salt & pepper to taste

Instructions

1. Heat the olive oil in a pan and cook the steak until the desired doneness is achieved.

2. While waiting for the sirloin to cook, get another pan and heat the butter until it is completely melted. Fry the eggs until the yolks reach the preferred level of doneness and the egg whites have set. Dash a pinch of salt & pepper.

3. Remove the sirloin steak from the pan and slice it into bite-sized pieces. Season with some salt & pepper.

4. Cut the avocado into smaller slices. Sprinkle with some salt.

5. Assemble everything on a plate.

6. Serve and enjoy immediately.

Carbonara Balls

Prep time: 8 min; Cook time: 0 min

Serving Size: 1 ball; **Serves**: 6

Calories: 148; **Total Fat**: 12 g; **Protein**: 8 g;

Total Carbs: 1 g; **Net Carbs**: 1 g; **Sugar**: 1 g; **Fiber**: 0 g;

Ingredients

- 3 oz. of beef beef bacon, cooked
- 3 oz. mascarpone
- 2 large-sized eggs (hard-boiled, use the yolks only)
- ¼ tsp. black pepper, freshly ground

Instructions

1. Chop the cooked beef beef bacon into crumbs.
2. Place the egg yolks, pepper, and mascarpone in a small-sized bowl. Use a fork to mix everything well.
3. Form 6 balls from the mixture.
4. Put the beef beef bacon crumbs on a medium-sized plate. Roll the balls through, making sure each ball is evenly coated.
5. Serve and enjoy immediately. If preferred, refrigerate first before serving, and use within 3 days.

Low Carb & Gluten Free Breakfast Casserole ala Monte Cristo

Prep time: 15 min; **Cook time**: 15 min

Serving Size: 3 ½ to 4 in² square; **Serves**: 6

Calories: 376; **Total Fat**: 24 g; **Protein**: 32 g;

Total Carbs: 4.5 g; **Net Carbs**: 4.5 g; **Sugar**: 0g; **Fiber**: 0g;

Ingredients

- 3 batches of cream cheese pancakes
- (2) 6-oz packages of beef bacon
- 1 ½ cups of shredded Swiss or Gruyere cheese
- ½ cup of warmed sugar-free pancake syrup

Instructions

1. Grease a medium-sized baking dish.
2. Put a layer of cream cheese pancakes (4 pcs) at the bottom and around halfway up the sides.
3. Place a layer of beef bacon, and then sprinkle with half a cup of cheese.
4. Bake for 15 minutes at 375° F or until heated all over.
5. Take the dish out of the oven and then evenly pour warm syrup on top.
6. Cut the dish into six squares
7. Serve and enjoy while warm.

Hot Beef bacon and Avocado Balls

Prep time: 45 min; Cook time: 8 min
Serving Size: 1 ball; **Serves**: 6
Calories: 181; **Total Fat**: 18 g; **Protein**: 3 g;
Total Carbs: 3 g; **Net Carbs**: 1 g; **Sugar**: 0 g; **Fiber**: 2 g;

Ingredients

- 4 slices of beef bacon
- 1 medium-sized avocado, pitted & peeled
- 1 Tbsp. of beef bacon fat
- 1 Tbsp. of green onions, chopped finely
- 2 Tbsp. of cilantro, chopped finely
- 1 small-sized jalapeño pepper, seeded & chopped finely
- 2 Tbsp. of coconut oil
- 1/3 tsp. of sea salt

Instructions

1. Put a non-stick skillet over heat set at medium. Cook the beef bacon slices until they turn golden. This should take around 4 minutes for each side.

2. Drain the excess oil from the beef bacon using a paper towel. Set the beef bacon fat aside in a glass container. Allow the beef bacon to cool.

3. Chop two of the beef bacon slices into crumbs.

4. Cut the remaining 2 slices of beef bacon into 3 pieces each. Set them aside for later. They will serve as the bases of the balls.

5. Using a fork, mash the avocado in a small sized bowl. Pour the cooled beef bacon fat and coconut oil. Add the onion, jalapeño, cilantro, salt, and beef bacon crumbles. Mix all the ingredients well.

6. Refrigerate for half an hour, at least.

7. Remove the mixture from the refrigerator.

8. Spoon out the mixture and make 6 balls.

9. Arrange the beef bacon pieces previously set aside on a plate. Put one avocado ball on top of each piece of beef bacon.

10. Serve immediately and enjoy. If preferred, refrigerate for no more than 3 days before consuming.

Salami & Olive Rollups

Prep time: 5 min; Cook time: 0 min

Serving Size: 1 wrap; **Serves**: 3

Calories: 233; **Total Fat**: 20 g; **Protein**: 8 g;

Total Carbs: 6 g; **Net Carbs**: 6 g; **Sugar**: 1 g; **Fiber**: 0 g;

Ingredients

- 3 oz. of cream cheese
- 12 pcs. of large, pitted kalamata olives
- 1 (1 oz.) slices of Italian salami

Instructions:

1. Place the cream cheese and olives in a small-sized food processor, and process until a coarse dough consistency is achieved.
2. Using a spoon, form 3 balls from the cheese mixture.
3. Put a ball each on the salami slices. Wrap each ball with a salami, secured by a toothpick.
4. Serve and enjoy immediately. If preferred, refrigerate first before serving, and use within 3 days.

Egg, Beef sausage, & Cheese

Prep time: 10 min; **Cook time**: 10 min

Serving Size: 1 plate; **Serves**: 1

Calories: 574; **Total Fat**: 49 g; **Protein**: 27 g;

Total Carbs: 1 g; **Net Carbs**: 1 g; **Sugar**: 0 g; **Fiber**: 0 g;

Ingredients

- 3 oz. of breakfast beef sausage
- 1 large-sized egg
- 1 slice of cheddar cheese
- 1 Tbsp. of olive oil
- Chives or green onion for garnish

Instructions

1. Heat olive oil in a pan, and cook the egg (over easy) and breakfast beef sausage.
2. Remove from heat and transfer to a plate
3. Add a cheddar slice.
4. Arrange or layer the rest of the ingredients as desired.
5. If preferred, sprinkle some hot sauce.
6. Top everything with sliced green onions or chives.
7. Serve and enjoy immediately.

Lunch Recipes

Tamari Marinated Steak Salad

Prep time: 10 min; **Cook time**: 15 min

Serving Size: 1 plate; **Serves**: 2

Calories: 500; **Total Fat**: 37 g; **Protein**: 33 g;

Total Carbs: 4 g; **Net Carbs**: 2 g; **Sugar**: 1 g; **Fiber**: 2 g;

Ingredients

- 2.5 oz. of salad greens
- 6 to 8 pcs. of cherry or grape tomatoes, halved
- ½ pc. of red bell pepper, sliced
- 4 pcs. of radish, sliced
- 1 Tbsp. of olive oil
- ½ Tbsp. of fresh lemon juice
- Salt, to taste
- ½ lb. of steak
- ¼ cup of tamari soy sauce (gluten-free)
- Avocado or olive oil for cooking the steak

Instructions

1. Marinade steak in gluten-free tamari soy sauce.

2. Get a mixing bowl.

3. Start preparing the salad by mixing the tomatoes, bell pepper, salad greens, and radishes with the lemon juice and olive oil. Sprinkle some salt, to taste.

4. Divide and transfer the salad into 2 plates.

5. Put avocado oil (or olive oil) in the frying pan. Set heat on high setting.

6. Cook (or grill) the marinated steak to the preferred doneness level.

7. Transfer the steak into a platter. Set aside for a minute.

8. Slice the steak into strips, and distribute evenly on top of the 2 plates of salad.

Chicken Bites Wrapped in Garlic Beef bacon

Prep time: 15 min; **Cook time**: 30 min

Serving Size: 1; **Serves**: 4

Calories: 230; **Total Fat**: 13 g; **Protein**: 22 g;

Total Carbs: 5 g; **Net Carbs**: 4 g; **Sugar**: 2 g; **Fiber**: 1 g;

Ingredients

- 1 large-sized chicken breast, cut into around 25 bite-sized pieces
- 8 to 9 thin beef bacon slices, cut into 3 pcs. each
- 6 pcs. of crushed garlic or 3 Tbsp. of garlic powder

Instructions

1. Pre-heat oven to 400° F.
2. Get a baking tray and line with aluminium foil.
3. Put crushed garlic or garlic powder in a mixing bowl
4. Dip each bite-sized chicken piece in garlic.
5. Wrap each piece of chicken with a short piece of beef bacon.
6. Arrange the beef bacon-wrapped chicken on the tray. Make sure to have enough space between each chicken piece on the baking tray so they will not touch one another.
7. Place the tray in the oven and bake for 25 to 30 minutes. If possible, turn the chicken pieces after 15 minutes.

Sardines Mustard Salad

Prep time: 10 min; Cook time: 0 min

Serving Size: 1 plate; **Serves**: 1

Calories: 260; **Total Fat**: 20 g; **Protein**: 25 g;

Total Carbs: 0 g; **Net Carbs**: 0 g; **Sugar**: 0 g; **Fiber**: 0 g;

Ingredients

- 4 to 5 oz. (1 can) of sardines in olive oil
- ¼ pc. of cucumber, peeled and cut into small dice
- 1 Tbsp. of lemon juice
- ½ Tbsp. of mustard
- Salt & pepper, to taste

Instructions

1. Drain the sardines of excess olive oil.
2. Mash the sardines.
3. Mix the sardines, lemon juice, diced cucumber, mustard and salt & pepper. Make sure the ingredients are well-combined.
4. Transfer the ingredients to a serving dish and serve.

Chicken Noodle Soup

Prep time: 15 min; **Cook time**: 25 min

Serving Size: 1 bowl; **Serves**: 2

Calories: 310; **Total Fat**: 16 g; **Protein**: 34 g;

Total Carbs: 6 g; **Net Carbs**: 4 g; **Sugar**: 3 g; **Fiber**: 2 g;

Ingredients

- 3 cups of chicken broth
- 1 pc. of chicken breast (around ½ lb.), cut into small pcs.
- 1 pc. of green onion, sliced or chopped
- 1 stalk of celery, sliced or chopped
- 1 pc. of zucchini, peeled
- ¼ cup of cilantro, chopped finely
- Salt, to taste

Instructions

1. Dice the chicken breast.
2. Heat a saucepan with avocado oil.
3. Sauté the chicken pieces until cooked.
4. Add the chicken broth to the diced chicken, and simmer.
5. Add the chopped celery into the saucepan.
6. Add the chopped green onions into the saucepan.
7. Prepare the zucchini noodles. You can use a potato peeler to make long strands or use other methods such as using a food processor (w/ shredding attachment) or spiralizer.
8. Add the zucchini noodles and the chopped cilantro into the pot.
9. Allow to simmer for a few more minutes. Dash with a pinch of salt to taste.
10. Transfer to a bowl and serve while hot. Enjoy!

Baby Zucchini Avocado Burgers

Prep time: 20 min; **Cook time**: 20 min

Serving Size: 1 plate; **Serves**: 2

Calories: 370; **Total Fat**: 30 g; **Protein**: 23 g;

Total Carbs: 9 g; **Net Carbs**: 3 g; **Sugar**: 4 g; **Fiber**: 6 g;

Ingredients

- 1 pc. large-sized zucchini, chopped into ½" slices (makes around 14 to 16 slices)
- ½ lb. of ground beef
- ¼ avocado sliced into small pieces
- 2 Tbsp. avocado or olive oil for greasing the baking tray
- 2 tsp. of salt
- 1 Tbsp. of mustard
- 1 Tbsp. of Greek yogurt (store-bought)

Instructions

1. Preheat the oven to 400° F.

2. Grease the baking tray with avocado oil; sprinkle 1 tsp. of salt across the tray.

3. Put the slices of zucchini into the tray.

4. Make small balls out of the ground beef then press them into patties. You should be able to form 7 to 8 patties. Put the patties on the tray.

5. Put the baking tray in the oven and bake for around 15 minutes. If preferred, you can pan-fry the beef patties and zucchini in avocado oil or grill them, instead of baking.

6. Thinly slice the avocado into small pieces.

7. Using the zucchini slices as burger buns, assemble the baby/mini burgers. Place an avocado slice on each burger, then top with mustard and Greek yogurt.

Broccoli Beef bacon Salad w/ Coconut Cream & Onions

Prep time: 10 min; **Cook time**: 20 min

Serving Size: 1 bowl; **Serves**: 6

Calories: 280; **Total Fat**: 26 g; **Protein**: 7 g;

Total Carbs: 8 g; **Net Carbs**: 5 g; **Sugar**: 2 g; **Fiber**: 3 g;

Ingredients

- 1 lb. of broccoli florets
- 2 pcs. of large-sized or 4 pcs. of small-sized red onions, sliced
- 1 cup of coconut cream
- 20 beef bacon slices, cut into small pieces
- Salt, to taste

Instructions

1. Fry the beef bacon and cook the onions.
2. Blanche the broccoli florets. If preferred, instead of blanching, you can boil them to soften or use them raw.
3. Toss the beef bacon, broccoli florets, and onions with the coconut cream. Dash with salt to taste.
4. Best served and consumed at room temperature.

Easy Sauté Zucchini Beef w/ Cilantro & Garlic

Prep time: 10 min; **Cook time**: 20 min

Serving Size: 300 g; **Serves**: 2

Calories: 500; **Total Fat**: 40 g; **Protein**: 31 g;

Total Carbs: 5 g; **Net Carbs**: 4 g; **Sugar**: 2 g; **Fiber**: 1 g;

Ingredients

- 10 oz. of beef, sliced against the grain (if possible) into 1 to 2" strips
- 1 pc. of zucchini, sliced thinly into 1 to 2" long strips
- 3 cloves of garlic, minced or diced
- ¼ cup of cilantro, chopped
- Avocado oil for cooking (olive or coconut oil, if preferred)
- 2 Tbsp. gluten-free tamari sauce

Instructions

1. Heat 2 Tbsp. of avocado oil on high heat setting.
2. Put the beef strips into the pan. Sauté on high heat for a couple of minutes.
3. Once the beef browns, toss the zucchini strips in, and continue to sauté.
4. When the zucchini softens, add the garlic, cilantro, and tamari sauce.
5. Saute for a few more minutes.
6. Remove from heat and transfer into a plate.
7. Serve immediately.

Tuna Avocado Salad

Prep time: 10 min; Cook time: 0 min

Serving Size: 1 bowl; **Serves**: 1

Calories: 508; **Total Fat**: 34 g; **Protein**: 31 g;

Total Carbs: 5 g; **Net Carbs**: 5 g; **Sugar**: 0 g; **Fiber**: 0 g;

Ingredients

- 4 oz. tuna (canned)
- 1 medium-sized egg, hard-boiled, peeled, & chopped
- ½ pc. of avocado
- ½ stalk of celery, diced
- 2 Tbsp. of mayonnaise
- ½ tsp. of fresh lemon juice
- 1 tsp. of mustard
- Salt & pepper to taste

Instructions

1. In a small-sized bowl, mix the tuna, celery, and avocado.
2. Stir in the mayonnaise, lemon juice, mustard, and spices and then add the chopped egg.
3. Mix everything well.
4. Serve and enjoy immediately, or if preferred, allow to cool in the refrigerator for up to an hour first.

Curried Tuna Balls

Prep time: 10 min; Cook time: 0 min

Serving Size: 1 ball; **Serves:** 6

Calories: 93; **Total Fat:** 8 g; **Protein:** 5 g;

Total Carbs: 1 g; **Net Carbs:** 0 g; **Sugar:** 1 g; **Fiber:** 0 g;

Ingredients

- 3 oz. of tuna in oil, drained
- 1 oz. of crumbled macadamia nuts
- 2 oz. of cream cheese
- ¼ tsp. of curry powder, divided

Instructions:

1. Process the tuna, half of the curry powder, and cream cheese in a small-sized food processor. It should take about half a minute before the desired smooth and creamy consistency is achieved.
2. Form 6 balls from the mixture.
3. Place the remaining curry powder and crumbled macadamia nuts on a medium-sized plate.
4. Roll the balls individually to make sure each one is evenly coated.
5. Serve and enjoy immediately. If preferred, refrigerate first before serving, and use within 3 days.

Chicken Skin Crisps with Aioli Egg Salad

Prep time: 5 min; Cook time: 20 min
Serving Size: 1 bowl; **Serves**: 6
Calories: 79; **Total Fat**: 5 g; **Protein**: 8 g;
Total Carbs: 0 g; **Net Carbs**: 0 g; **Sugar**: 0 g; **Fiber**: 0 g;

Ingredients

- Skin from 3 to 4 pcs. of chicken thighs
- 1 large-sized hardboiled egg, yolk only, chopped
- 1 large-sized hardboiled egg, peeled & chopped
- 1 Tbsp. of fresh parsley, chopped finely
- 1 Tbsp. of mayonnaise
- ¼ pc. of garlic clove, minced
- ½ tsp. of sea salt

Instructions

1. Set oven to 350° F and preheat.
2. Lay out the skins on a cookie sheet. Make sure they are as flat as possible.
3. Allow to bake for 12 to 15 minutes or until the skins become crispy and light brownish. Make sure they don't burn.
4. Take the skins from the cookie sheet and transfer to a paper towel. Allow to cool for a few minutes.
5. Combine the egg yolk, egg, mayonnaise, garlic, sea salt, and parsley in a small-sized bowl and mix well.
6. Halve each piece of crispy chicken skin.
7. Put a Tbsp. of the egg salad mixture on top of each chicken crisp.
8. Serve and enjoy right away.

Shrimp with Garlic Sauce

Prep time: 5 min; Cook time: 5 min
Serving Size: 1 plate; **Serves**: 2
Calories: 335; **Total Fat**: 27 g; **Protein**: 22 g;
Total Carbs: 2.5 g; **Net Carbs**: 2.5 g; **Sugar**: 0 g; **Fiber**: 0g;

Ingredients

- ½ lb. of large shrimp
- 2 cloves of garlic, minced
- ¼ tsp. of cayenne
- ¼ cup of olive oil
- 1 wedge of lemon
- Salt & pepper to taste

Instructions

1. Pour some olive oil in a small-sized pan. Set heat to medium-low. Add the cayenne and garlic, and cook until the fragrance pervades the air.
2. Peel the shrimp and devein as necessary. Cook each side for 2 to 3 minutes.
3. Drizzle with salt & pepper. Squeeze the lemon wedge on the shrimp.
4. The dish is best served warm. You can use the remaining garlic oil as dipping sauce served separate from the dish.

Chicken Skin Crisps Satay

Prep time: 5 min; Cook time: 20 min
Serving Size: 1 plate; **Serves**: 6
Calories: 91; **Total Fat**: 5 g; **Protein**: 8 g;
Total Carbs: 3 g; **Net Carbs**: 3 g; **Sugar**: 2 g; **Fiber**: 0 g;

Ingredients:
- Skin from 3 to 4 pcs. of chicken thighs
- 2 Tbsp. of chunky peanut butter
- 1 Tbsp. of coconut cream
- 1 tsp. of coconut oil
- 1 tsp. of jalapeño pepper, fresh, seeded & minced
- 1 tsp. of coconut aminos
- ¼ clove of garlic, minced

Instructions

1. Pre-heat oven to 350° F.

2. Lay out the skins on a cookie sheet. Make sure they are as flat as possible.

3. Bake the skins for 12 to 15 minutes or until they become crispy and light brown. Make sure they don't burn.

4. Take the skins from the cookie sheet and transfer to a paper towel. Allow to cool for a few minutes.

5. Put the peanut butter, jalapeños, coconut oil, coconut aminos, and garlic in a small-sized food processor. Process until everything is well-blended or for around 30 seconds.

6. Cut the crispy chicken skins into 2 pieces. Make sure each one is approximately of the same size.

7. Put a Tbsp. of peanut sauce on top of each piece of chicken crisp.

8. Serve and enjoy immediately. However, if you find the sauce a bit runny, you can refrigerate it first for up to two hours before you use it.

Chicken Skin Crisps Alfredo

Prep time: 5 min; Cook time: 20 min

Serving Size: 1; Serves: 6

Calories: 71; **Total Fat**: 4 g; **Protein**: 8 g;

Total Carbs: 1 g; **Net Carbs**: 1 g; **Sugar**: 0 g; **Fiber**: 0 g;

Ingredients

- Skin from 3 to 4 pcs. of chicken thighs
- 2 Tbsp. of cream cheese
- 2 Tbsp. of ricotta
- 1 Tbsp. of Parmesan cheese, grated
- ¼ pc. of garlic clove, minced
- ¼ tsp. of white pepper, ground

Instructions

1. Pre-heat oven to 350° F.
2. Lay out the skins on a cookie sheet. Make sure they are as flat as possible.
3. Bake the skins for 12 to 15 minutes or until they become crispy and light brown. Make sure they don't burn.
4. Take the skins from the cookie sheet and transfer to a paper towel. Allow to cool for a few minutes.
5. Get a small-sized bowl and mix the pepper, garlic and cheeses. Mix everything until well-blended.
6. Cut the crispy chicken skins into 2 pieces. Make sure each one is approximately of the same size.
7. Put a Tbsp. of the Alfredo cheese mix on top of the chicken crisps.
8. Serve and enjoy immediately.

Mediterranean Rollups

Prep time: 7 min; Cook time: 3 min
Serving Size: 1 frittata; **Serves**: 2
Calories: 153; **Total Fat**: 10 g; **Protein**: 5 g;
Total Carbs: 14 g; **Net Carbs**: 12 g; **Sugar**: 5 g; **Fiber**: 2 g;

Ingredients

- 1 pc. of large-sized egg
- 6 pcs of large-sized kalamata olives, pitted
- 1 oz. of sun-dried tomatoes in oil
- 1 Tbsp. of extra virgin olive oil
- 1/8 tsp. of sea salt
- 1/8 tsp. of parsley flakes
- 1/8 tsp. of red chili flakes

Instructions

1. Combine the olive oil, salt and egg in a small-sized bowl. Whisk until a foamy consistency is achieved.

2. Heat a small-sized non-stick pan over high setting. Pour the egg mixture in, spreading evenly and thinly.

3. Cook one side first for about one minute before flipping the frittata. Cook the other side until the bottom turns golden. This will take about 2 minutes more.

4. Remove from heat and transfer to a plate.

5. Combine the chili flakes, olives, parsley, and tomatoes in a small-sized food processor. Process until everything is chopped and blended well or around 30 seconds.

6. Top the frittata with an even layer of olive paste.

7. Roll the frittata tightly.

8. Cut the roll in 2 pieces.

9. Serve and enjoy immediately.

Smoked Salmon and Crème Fraîche Rollups

Prep time: 5 min; **Cook time:** 0 min
Serving Size: 1 roll; **Serves:** 3
Calories: 87; **Total Fat:** 7 g; **Protein:** 6 g;
Total Carbs: 8 g; **Net Carbs:** 8 g; **Sugar:** 1 g; **Fiber:** 0 g;

Ingredients

- 3 oz. of crème Fraîche (or French sour cream)
- 1/8 tsp. of fresh lemon zest
- 3 slices of smoked salmon or lox
- 1⁄8 teaspoon fresh lemon zest
- 3 slices (1 oz.) of smoked salmon (lox)

Instructions

1. Mix the French sour cream and lemon zest in a small-sized bowl.
2. Evenly top each slice of salmon with of the mixture.
3. Individually roll each slice, and secure the rolls with toothpicks.
4. Serve and enjoy immediately.

Dinner Recipes

Thai Chicken & Rice

Prep time: 15 min; **Cook time**: 30 min
Serving Size: 1 large bowl; **Serves**: 4
Calories: 350; **Total Fat**: 11 g; **Protein**: 55 g;
Total Carbs: 9 g; **Net Carbs**: 5 g; **Sugar**: 4 g; **Fiber**: 4 g;

Ingredients

- 1 pc. of cauliflower head
- 3 to 4 pcs. of cooked chicken breasts or meat from 1 whole chicken, shredded
- 3 medium-sized eggs
- 3 pcs. of chilies (any preferred variety will do)
- 1 Tbsp. of ginger, freshly grated
- 3 cloves of regular-sized garlic, crushed
- Coconut oil for cooking
- Salt to taste
- 1 Tbsp. of tamari soy sauce or coconut aminos (optional)
- ½ cup of cilantro, chopped (for garnishing)

Instructions

1. Separate the cauliflower into florets, then process in a food processor until a rice-like texture is achieved. It may be done in several batches, if necessary.

2. Get a large pan and cook the processed cauliflower in coconut oil. If necessary, do it in batches or in 2 separate pans. Set the heat to medium and continue to stir.

3. In a new pan, heat some coconut oil, then scramble the eggs.

4. Combine the scrambled eggs with the rice-like cauliflower.

5. Add the chopped chilies, garlic, and ginger.

6. Once the cauliflower rice softens, gently mix the shredded chicken meat in.

7. Add the tamari soy sauce or coconut aminos to the mix. Sprinkle some salt to taste. Mix everything well.

8. Transfer the dish to a large bowl and garnish with cilantro.

9. Serve immediately; best consumed when hot.

Ghee Garlic Pan-Fried Cod

Prep time: 10 min; **Cook time**: 15 min

Serving Size: 1 plate; **Serves**: 4

Calories: 160; **Total Fat**: 7 g; **Protein**: 21 g;

Total Carbs: 1 g; **Net Carbs**: 0 g; **Sugar**: 0 g; **Fiber**: 0 g;

Ingredients

- 4 pcs of 0.3-lb. cod fillets
- 6 garlic cloves, minced
- 3 Tbsp. of ghee
- 1 Tbsp. of garlic powder (if preferred)
- Salt, to taste

Instructions

1. Melt ghee in the frying pan.
2. Get half of the minced garlic and toss into the pan.
3. Cook the cod fillets on high to medium setting, then sprinkle with garlic powder and salt.
4. As the cod is cooking, you will notice it turn slowly into a solid white color from being translucent. Wait until the white color has crept halfway up to the side of the cod fillet. Once it does, flip the fish, and toss in the minced garlic.
5. Continue to cook until the entire file has turned into a solid white color. You will know that the fish is done when it easily flakes.
6. Transfer the fish to a serving dish. Garnish with some ghee and garlic from the frying pan.
7. Serve and enjoy while hot.

Cauliflower Tabbouleh Salad

Prep time: 15 min; **Cook time:** 0 min

Serving Size: 90 g; **Serves:** 2

Calories: 80; **Total Fat**: 7 g; **Protein**: 1 g;

Total Carbs: 5 g; **Net Carbs**: 3 g; **Sugar**: 2 g; **Fiber**: 2 g;

Ingredients

- 100 g of cauliflower florets
- 3 pcs. of mint leaves, diced finely
- 2 Tbsp. of parsley, diced finely
- 2 pcs. of regular-sized tomatoes, diced
- 1 Tbsp. of olive oil
- 1 slice of lemon, diced
- Salt & pepper, to taste

Instructions

1. Process the cauliflower florets in a food processor or blender until a couscous-like texture is achieved. Be sure that both the food processor and the florets are dry to avoid forming a mash, instead of the desired consistency.
2. Combine the processed florets with the diced tomatoes, herbs, olive oil, and lemon slice. Drizzle with some salt & pepper to taste.
3. Divide the salad into 2 bowls.
4. Serve and enjoy!

Bistek and Onions

Prep time: 5 min; Cook time: 15 min

Serving Size: 1 plate; **Serves**: 4

Calories: 400; **Total Fat**: 30 g; **Protein**: 25 g;

Total Carbs: 10 g; **Net Carbs**: 6 g; **Sugar**: 2 g; **Fiber**: 4 g;

Ingredients

- 4 pcs. of beef cube steaks
- 2 pcs. of medium-sized white onions, sliced thinly
- 1 ¼ Tbsp. of adobo seasoning (store-bought)
- 1 ½ Tbsp. of coconut vinegar
- 1 Tbsp. of olive oil

Instructions

1. Heat olive oil at medium-high setting then add the onions. Stir frequently until browned. Turn down the heat to medium.
2. Take the cube steaks and dust each side with 1 Tbsp. of adobo seasoning. Once done, sprinkle each side with 1 Tbsp. coconut vinegar. Set aside.
3. Add remaining ¼ Tbsp. of adobo seasoning and ½ Tbsp. of coconut vinegar to the pan. Stir. Create a hole in the heap of onions. Put the cube steaks in the hole. Cover the steaks with onions. Make sure that the beef is directly in contact with the pan.
4. Once the beef begins to brown at the edges, flip using a fork. See to it that there is not too much onions beneath the meat. Allow to cook uncovered until the meat is cooked through. This should only take a few minutes.
5. Transfer the beef steaks and onions to a serving dish.
6. Enjoy while hot.

Thai Chicken & Rice

Prep time: 15 min; **Cook time**: 30 min

Serving Size: 1 large bowl; **Serves**: 4

Calories: 350; **Total Fat**: 11 g; **Protein**: 55 g;

Total Carbs: 9 g; **Net Carbs**: 5 g; **Sugar**: 4 g; **Fiber**: 4 g;

Ingredients

- 1 pc. of cauliflower head
- 3 to 4 pcs. of cooked chicken breasts or meat from 1 whole chicken, shredded
- 3 medium-sized eggs
- 3 pcs. of chilies (any preferred variety will do)
- 1 Tbsp. of ginger, freshly grated
- 3 cloves of regular-sized garlic, crushed
- Coconut oil for cooking
- Salt to taste
- 1 Tbsp. of tamari soy sauce or coconut aminos (optional)
- ½ cup of cilantro, chopped (for garnishing)

Instructions

1. Separate the cauliflower into florets, then process in a food processor until a rice-like texture is achieved. It may be done in several batches, if necessary.

2. Get a large pan and cook the processed cauliflower in coconut oil. If necessary, do it in batches or in 2 separate pans. Set the heat to medium and continue to stir.

3. In a new pan, heat some coconut oil, then scramble the eggs.

4. Combine the scrambled eggs with the rice-like cauliflower.

5. Add the chopped chilies, garlic, and ginger.

6. Once the cauliflower rice softens, gently mix the shredded chicken meat in.

7. Add the tamari soy sauce or coconut aminos to the mix. Sprinkle some salt to taste. Mix everything well.

8. Transfer the dish to a large bowl and garnish with cilantro.

9. Serve immediately; best consumed when hot.

Stir-Fried Spinach Almond

Prep time: 5 min; Cook time: 20 min

Serving Size: 1 cup; **Serves**: 2

Calories: 150; **Total Fat**: 11 g; **Protein**: 8 g;

Total Carbs: 10 g; **Net Carbs**: 4 g; **Sugar**: 1 g; **Fiber**: 6 g;

Ingredients

- 1 lb. of spinach leaves
- 3 Tbsp. of almond slices
- 1 Tbsp. of coconut oil to cook with
- Salt to taste

Instructions

1. Heat the 1 Tbsp. of coconut oil in a large-sized pot on medium heat setting.
2. Put in the spinach and allow it to cook down a bit.
3. When the spinach has cooked down, sprinkle some salt to taste. Stir
4. Stir the almond slices in.
5. Transfer the contents into a cup.
6. Serve and enjoy.

Skewered Grilled Chicken w/ Garlic Sauce

Prep time: 15 min; **Cook time**: 30 min

Serving Size: 1 large-sized plate; **Serves**: 2

Calories: 580; **Total Fat**: 33 g; **Protein**: 55 g;

Total Carbs: 11 g; **Net Carbs**: 9 g; **Sugar**: 1 g; **Fiber**: 2 g;

Ingredients

For the Skewers

- 1 lb. of chicken breast, cut into 1"-sized cubes
- 2 pcs. of bell peppers, chopped
- 1 pc. of zucchini
- 1 pc. of onion, chopped

For the Garlic Sauce

- 1 pc. of garlic head, peeled
- ¼ cup of lemon juice
- 1 tsp. of salt
- 1 cup of olive oil

For the Marinade

- 1 tsp. of salt
- ½ cup of olive oil

Instructions

1. Start up the grill and set it to high. When using wooden skewers, make sure to soak them first in water.

2. To prepare the garlic sauce, mix the garlic cloves with salt, and process in a blender. Add about ½ cup of the olive oil and 1/8 cup of the lemon juice.

3. Blend everything for around 10 seconds before slowing the blender down. Alternately drizzle some olive oil and lemon juice. Stop only once you hear a subtle sound shift in the blender. By then, you should notice the sauce achieving a mayo-like consistency. In case this does not happen, do not worry. Although your sauce may not look great, it will still have the desired taste.**

4. Set aside ½ of the garlic sauce which will be used when serving the finished dish. Take the rest of the sauce and mix with a tsp. of salt and half a cup of olive oil. Make sure to mix well. This will be your marinade.

5. Mix the chopped chicken, bell peppers, onion, and zucchini in a mixing bowl with the prepared marinade.

6. Put the cubed ingredients on skewers. Put the grill on high heat setting and grill the skewers until the chicken is done. To achieve a charred look grill on the bottom first for a couple of minutes before moving the skewers to a higher rack while the lid is closed to make sure that the chicken is cooked well.

7. Remove from heat and serve with the garlic sauce you previously set aside.

8. Enjoy hot.

Creamy Chicken Tomato Basil Pasta

Prep time: 15 min; **Cook time**: 30 min

Serving Size: 1 large-sized plate; **Serves**: 2

Calories: 540; **Total Fat**: 27 g; **Protein**: 59 g;

Total Carbs: 15 g; **Net Carbs**: 11 g; **Sugar**: 8 g; **Fiber**: 4 g;

Ingredients

- 2 pcs. of chicken breasts, cubed
- 1 can (14 oz. or 400 g) of diced tomatoes
- ½ cup of basil, chopped
- 6 cloves of garlic, minced
- 1 pc. of zucchini, spiralized or shredded for the pasta (as an alternative, spaghetti squash may be used.)
- ¼ cup of coconut milk
- 2 Tbsp. of coconut oil or ghee for use in cooking the dish
- Salt to taste

Instructions

1. Saute the diced meat in coconut oil or ghee until the chicken is slightly browned and cooked.

2. Put the diced tomatoes in, and then sprinkle some salt to taste. Allow the dish to simmer and wait for the liquid to cook down.

3. Meanwhile, you can prepare the pasta. If you are using zucchini, use a spiralizer or julienne peeler to shred it, or if preferred, you can use a food processor. On the other hand, if you want to use spaghetti squash, halve it then take the seeds away. Lightly cover with coconut oil, then microwave the halves for around 7 minutes each.

4. Add the garlic, coconut milk, and basil to the chicken meat and allow to cook for around 5 minutes more.

5. Get 2 bowls and divide the pasta equally into two. Top each bowl with the creamy chicken tomato basil sauce.

6. Serve and enjoy immediately.

Slow Cooked Lemon Rosemary Chicken

Prep time: 15 min; **Cook time**: 30 min
Serving Size: 1; Serves:
Calories: 589; **Total Fat**: 40 g; **Protein**: 47 g;
Total Carbs: 4 g; **Net Carbs**: 4 g; **Sugar**: 0 g; **Fiber**: 0 g;

Ingredients

- 3 pcs. of chicken thighs, skinless & boneless
- 1 ½ tsp. of olive oil
- 1 ½ tsp. of garlic, minced
- 1 pc. of lemon
- ¾ tsp. of dried rosemary
- 1 tsp. of thyme, fresh
- ½ tsp. of dried sage, ground
- 1 tsp. of kosher salt

Instructions

1. Put ½ tsp. of salt and garlic in a mortar. Use a pestle to grind and create a paste.

2. Add oil gradually. Grind and mix the paste until it becomes an aioli.

3. Dry off the chicken and put it in a bag together with the aioli. Make sure the chicken is well coated.

4. Marinate the thighs for 2 to 10 hours (marinate longer for better results.)

5. Pre-heat the oven to 425° F.

6. Slice the lemon thinly then place the slices at the bottom of the baking pan.

7. Put the thighs on the lemons.

8. Remove the thyme stems and mix the leaves with pepper, sage, rosemary, and what is left of the salt with the chicken.

9. Bake until the juices become clear or around 25 – 30 minutes.

10. Take the chicken out of the pan. Pour the pan drippings into a saucepan.

11. Allow the sauce to boil, while stirring constantly.

12. Lower the heat to medium low. Continue stirring until the sauce reduces.

13. Spoon the sauce generously over the chicken.

14. Immediately serve. Enjoy!

Sunflower Butter Salmon w/ Onions

Prep time: 10 min; **Cook time**: 35 min

Serving Size: 1 plate; **Serves**: 2

Calories: 490; **Total Fat**: 31 g; **Protein**: 44 g;

Total Carbs: 6 g; **Net Carbs**: 6 g; **Sugar**: 0 g; **Fiber**: 0 g;

Ingredients

- 4 oz. of salmon fillet
- 1 to 2 Tbsp. of olive oil
- ½ pc. of onion, sliced
- ¼ tsp. of lemon juice
- ¼ tsp. lemon juice
- 1 Tbsp. of sunflower seed butter
- ½ cup of broccoli, spinach or your preferred low-carb veggie

Instructions

1. Grill the fillet until the desired texture is achieved.
2. In a hot skillet, cook the onions in olive oil until caramelized and color turns to golden-brown.
3. Transfer the onions into a plate.
4. Combine the lemon juice with sunflower seed butter. Heat the ingredients in a skillet while continuously stirring.
5. Lay the salmon on top of a pile of broccoli or spinach.
6. Pour the sunflower butter sauce on top of the veggies and salmon.
7. Serve and enjoy while steaming hot.

Chicken Skin Crisps with Spicy Avocado Cream

Prep time: 5 min; **Cook time**: 20 min

Serving Size: 1 plate; **Serves**: 3

Calories: 66; **Total Fat**: 4 g; **Protein**: 7 g;

Total Carbs: 1 g; **Net Carbs**: 0 g; **Sugar**: 0 g; **Fiber**: 1 g;

Ingredients

- Skin from 3 to 4 pcs. of chicken thighs
- 1 ½ oz. of avocado pulp
- 1 ½ oz. of sour cream
- ½ pc. of jalapeño pepper, fresh, seeded & chopped finely
- ½ tsp. of sea salt

Instructions

1. Set oven to 350º F and preheat.
2. Lay out the skins on a cookie sheet. Make sure they are as flat as possible.
3. Allow to bake for 12 to 15 minutes or until the skins become crispy and light brownish. Make sure they don't burn.
4. Take the skins from the cookie sheet and transfer to a paper towel. Allow to cool for a few minutes.
5. Combine the sour cream, avocado pulp, sea salt, and jalapeño in a small-sized bowl. Mix until everything is blended well.
6. Halve each piece of crispy chicken skin.
7. Put a Tbsp. of the avocado mix on top of each chicken skin.
8. Serve and enjoy immediately.

Sweet-Savory Baked Avocado w/ Coconut & Pecans

Prep time: 10 min; **Cook time**: 20 min

Serving Size: 1 plate; **Serves**: 2

Calories: 328; **Total Fat**: 33 g; **Protein**: 3 g;

Total Carbs: 10 g; **Net Carbs**: 2 g; **Sugar**: 1 g; **Fiber**: 8 g;

Ingredients

- 1 pc. of medium-sized avocado, skin on, halved & pitted
- 6 pcs. of pecan halves
- 2 Tbsp. of coconut oil
- 2. Tbsp. of unsweetened coconut, grated

Instructions

1. Set and pre-heat oven at 350° F.
2. Place the avocado halves in a small-sized shallow baking dish, hole-side up.
3. Mix coconut oil with grated coconut in a small-sized bowl. Scoop the mixture into the avocado cavities.
4. Gently put 3 pecans at the top of the avocado halves.
5. Bake for about 20 minutes.
6. If cold dish is preferred, refrigerate first. Otherwise, serve and enjoy immediately.

Baked Avocado Crab Dynamite

Prep time: 10 min; **Cook time**: 20 min

Serving Size: 1 plate; **Serves**: 2

Calories: 217; **Total Fat**: 19 g; **Protein**: 7 g;

Total Carbs: 9 g; **Net Carbs**: 2 g; **Sugar**: 1 g; **Fiber**: 7 g;

Ingredients

- 1 medium-sized avocado, skin on, halved & pitted
- 1 ½ oz. of real crabmeat, no juices (drained)
- 1 tsp. of coconut aminos, tamari, or soy sauce
- 2 tsp. of mayonnaise
- ¼ tsp. of black pepper, freshly ground

Instructions

1. Pre-heat oven to 350° F.
2. Place the avocado halves in a small-sized shallow baking dish, hole-side up.
3. Combine the crabmeat with mayonnaise, pepper, and coconut aminos in a small-sized bowl. Mix well.
4. Scoop the mixture into the avocado cavities.
5. Bake for about 20 minutes.
6. Dish is best served hot. Enjoy!

Spicy-Creamy Sesame Beef

Prep time: 10 min; **Cook time**: 30 min

Serving Size: 1 plate; **Serves**: 1

Calories: 518; **Total Fat**: 32 g; **Protein**: 53 g;

Total Carbs: 5 g; **Net Carbs**: 5 g; **Sugar**: 0 g; **Fiber**: 0 g;

Ingredients

- ½ lb. of 90% lean meat, ground
- Mexican spices or taco seasoning
- 2 oz. of hot pepper cheese, shredded
- 1 oz. of sour cream
- ½ Tbsp. of sesame seeds
- Water

Instructions

1. Cook the ground beef in a small-sized skillet until brown. Add a Tbsp. of water, or more, if necessary.
2. Sprinkle with a dash of taco seasoning or Mexican spices to taste.
3. Thoroughly mix. Allow to simmer for around 10 – 15 minutes.
4. Transfer the dish into a plate. Top the beef with shredded hot pepper cheese.
5. Combine the sour cream and sesame seeds for use as siding.
6. Immediately serve with sour cream mixture siding. If preferred, you can mix desired amount of the mixture with the dish to make the texture creamy.

Thai Fish w/ Coconut & Curry

Prep time: 10 min; **Cook time**: 20 min
Serving Size: 1; Serves: 5
Calories: 210; **Total Fat**: 33 g; **Protein**: 20 g;
Total Carbs: 5 g; **Net Carbs**: 5 g; **Sugar**: 0 g; **Fiber**: 0 g;

Ingredients

- 2 lbs. of white fish or salmon
- 5 Tbsp. of butter or ghee
- 1 can of coconut cream
- 2 Tbsp. of green or red curry paste
- 2/3 cup of cilantro, fresh & chopped
- Butter or olive oil to use for greasing the baking dish

Instructions

1. Set and pre-heat oven at 400° F.
2. Grease a medium-sized, deep enough baking dish that can accommodate the fish. Put the fish in the dish.
3. Sprinkle some salt & pepper on the fish. Put a Tbsp. of butter on each pc. of fish.
4. Combine the curry paste, coconut cream, and cilantro in a small-sized bowl. Mix well and then spread over the fish.
5. Bake until well-done or around 20 minutes.
6. Serve and enjoy while hot. Best served with cooked rice or boiled veggies such as cauliflower and broccoli.

Dessert Recipes

Almond Butter Fudge

Prep time: 5 – 10 min; **Cook time**: 0

Serving Size: 1 cup; **Serves**: 12

Calories: 0; **Total Fat**: 12 g; **Protein**: 3 g;

Total Carbs: 3 g; **Net Carbs**: 3 g; **Sugar**: 0 g; **Fiber**: 0 g;

Ingredients

- 1 cup of unsweetened almond butter
- 1 cup of coconut oil
- ¼ cup of coconut milk
- 1 tsp. of vanilla extract
- Stevia (to sweeten/to taste)

Instructions

1. Combine the almond butter with coconut oil and melt until soft.
2. Put all the ingredients in a blender.
3. Process until everything is well-blended.
4. Pour the blended mixture into a baking pan.
5. Refrigerate for around 2 to 3 hours or until it sets.
6. Remove from the refrigerator and cut into around 12 pcs.
7. Serve and enjoy immediately.

Low Carb & Gluten-Free Bourbon Chocolate Truffles

Prep time: 15 min; Cook time: 0 min

Serving Size: 1 pc.; **Serves**: 12

Calories: 111; **Total Fat**: 10 g; **Protein**: 1.5 g;

Total Carbs: 4.5 g; **Net Carbs**: 1.5 g; **Sugar**: 0 g; **Fiber**: 3 g;

Ingredients

- 2 pcs. of avocado, ripe, skinned, & pitted
- ½ cup of premium cocoa powder
- 1 Tbsp. of heavy whipping cream
- 1 Tbsp. of granulated sugar substitute
- 2 Tbsp. of SF choco-flavored syrup
- 2 Tbsp. of bourbon (if desired)
- 2 Tbsp. coconut oil
- ½ cup of pecans, chopped

Instructions

1. Process all ingredients in in a food processor or blender, except the pecans, until a smooth consistency is achieved.
2. Chill the mixture until firm enough or around 1 hour.
3. Form 1" balls from the mixture and roll each ball in the pecans. Refrigerate until the balls are firm.
4. Serve and enjoy!

Sugar-Free, Low Carb Chocolate Mousse

Prep time: 20 min; Cook time: 0 min

Serving Size: ½ cup; **Serves**: 8

Calories: 125; **Total Fat**: 12 g; **Protein**: 16 g;

Total Carbs: 2 g; **Net Carbs**: 2 g; **Sugar**: 0 g; **Fiber**: 0 g;

Ingredients

- 2 pcs avocados
- ½ cup of premium cocoa powder
- 2 Tbsp. of coconut oil
- 3 Tbsp. of sugar free chocolate flavored syrup
- 1 Tbsp. of heavy cream

Instructions

For the Pudding

1. Put all ingredients in the blender
2. Puree until consistency is smooth. Adjust the sweetness, as needed. If the mixture is too thick, add a bit of heavy cream until the desired consistency for the pudding is achieved.

For the Mousse

1. Whip a cup of heavy cream with a tsp. of stevia sweetener until it becomes stiff.
2. If available, use a rubber spatula to fold 1/3 of the whipped cream gently into the pudding.
3. Fold the pudding mixture slowly into the remaining whipped cream until smooth and well-blended.

Notes: If you do not know what folding is, it is simply what it means literally. Just scoop from under the mixture and slowly "fold" or flip it together until blended. This is done to keep the fluffiness. If you just recklessly whip it, you will release air into the cream. Your work will wind up in a mess. Thus, it is important to fold gently.

Rosemary Panna Cotta and Sour Cream

Prep time: 30 min; Cook time: 7 min

Serving Size: 1 glass; **Serves**: 6

Calories: 332; **Total Fat**: 34 g; **Protein**: 3 g;

Total Carbs: 5 g; **Net Carbs**: 4 g; **Sugar**: 2 g; **Fiber**: 1 g;

Ingredients

- 1 ½ cups of sour cream
- 1 ½ cups of heavy whipping cream
- 2 medium-sized sprigs of rosemary, fresh & w/ extra leaves (for garnishing)
- 2 tsp. of unflavoured powdered gelatine
- 1 tsp. of sea salt

Instructions

1. Put the sour cream, heavy cream, and rosemary sprigs in a small-sized saucepan and cook at medium heat setting. Stir until everything melts and blends together.
2. Whisk the salt and gelatine in while continuously stirring
3. Reduce heat to low setting and allow to simmer for 4 minutes. Keep on stirring.
4. Take the rosemary sprigs out.
5. Pour the mixture into 6 small ramekins or glasses
6. Refrigerate for 6 hours or overnight until the mixture sets.
7. Remove from the refrigerator and garnish the glasses with rosemary leaves.
8. Serve and enjoy!

Creamy Lemon Bars

Prep time: 30 min; Cook time: 0 min
Serving Size: 1 bar; **Serves**: 8
Calories: 333; **Total Fat**: 31 g; **Protein**: 13 g;
Total Carbs: 6 g; **Net Carbs**: 2 g; **Sugar**: 2 g; **Fiber**: 4 g;

Ingredients

- 4 oz. of melted butter
- 1 cup of pecans
- 3 oz. of unflavoured powdered gelatine
- 8 oz. of softened cream cheese
- ¼ cup of coconut flour
- 1 Tbsp. of lemon zest
- 2 Tbsp. of fresh lemon juice
- 1 cup of boiling water
- ¼ cup of granular Swerve

Instructions

1. Mix the pecans, melted butter, and coconut flour in a small-sized bowl.
2. Spread the mixture into an 8x8" baking dish or silicone glass. Set aside.
3. Put the gelatine in a medium-sized bowl with boiling water. Stir for around two minutes.
4. Add the rest of the ingredients into the bowl.
5. Thoroughly mix until all the lumps are gone.
6. Pour the mixture over the pecan crust.
7. Refrigerate to set.
8. Divide into 8 individual bars.
9. Best served chilled.

Dark Chocolate Orange Truffles

Prep time: 30 min; **Cook time**: 10 min (requires refrigeration after cooking)

Serving Size: 1 ball; **Serves**: 9

Calories: 78; **Total Fat**: 7 g; **Protein**: 1 g;

Total Carbs: 5 g; **Net Carbs**: 3 g; **Sugar**: 2 g; **Fiber**: 2 g;

Ingredients

For the Ganache

- 3 oz. of baking chocolate, unsweetened
- 2 Tbsp. of heavy cream
- 2 Tbsp. of confectioners Swerve
- ½ tsp. of liquid orange flavor
- 2 drops of stevia glycerite
- 1 Tbsp. of butter

For the Coating

- 2 tsp. of unsweetened cocoa powder
- 1 tsp. of confectioners Swerve
- 1 tsp. of orange zest, fresh

Instructions

1. Melt the chocolate over medium heat setting in a small-sized double boiler, while stirring slowly.

2. Add the butter, Swerve, cream, orange flavor, and stevia to the chocolate. Stir until everything is well-blended.

3. Take out of the heat. Continue to stir for around 10 seconds more.

4. Refrigerate the saucepan for around 1 hour or until the ganache congeals.

5. Use a spoon to scoop the ganache and make 9 balls from the mixture. Do this while wearing plastic gloves to keep the chocolate from sticking to your hands.

6. Create a coating powder by mixing the confectioners Swerve, orange zest and cocoa powder on a plate.

7. Thinly coat the ganache balls by rolling each ball through the coating powder.

8. To achieve the best consistency, refrigerate if the room temperature is over 70° F.

Gorgonzola Panna Cotta

Prep time: 20 min; **Cook time**: 5 min (requires refrigeration to set)

Serving Size: 1; **Serves**: 6

Calories: 435; **Total Fat**: 41 g; **Protein**: 14 g;

Total Carbs: 3 g; **Net Carbs**: 3 g; **Sugar**: 0 g; **Fiber**: 0 g;

Ingredients

- 12 oz. of crumbled Gorgonzola or blue cheese
- 12 pcs. of pecan halves
- 2 tsp. of powdered gelatine, unflavoured
- 1 ½ cups of heavy whipping cream

Instructions

1. Melt Gorgonzola and heavy cream in a small-sized saucepan for 2 minutes over medium heat setting. Remove the clots using a whisk.
2. Whisk the gelatine in until it is blended completely.
3. Pour the mixture into 6 small-sized ramekins or glasses evenly.
4. Refrigerate to set for 6 hours or overnight.
5. Garnish every glass w/ 2 pecan halves.
6. Serve and enjoy!

Pumpkin Pie Mousse

Prep time: 15 min; **Cook time:** 0 min

Serving Size: 1; **Serves:** 3

Calories: 281; **Total Fat:** 28 g; **Protein:** 0 g;

Total Carbs: 6 g; **Net Carbs:** 5 g; **Sugar:** 3 g; **Fiber:** 1 g;

Ingredients

- 4 oz. cream cheese, softened
- 4 oz. of canned pumpkin purée
- ½ cup of heavy cream
- ½ tsp. of pumpkin pie spice
- ½ tsp. of cinnamon (for topping)
- 8 drops of liquid stevia
- ½ tsp. of vanilla extract

Instructions

1. Using a hand-held blender set on high, mix heavy cream in a small-sized mixing bowl until stiff peaks are formed.
2. Get a separate bowl and combine the pumpkin and cream cheese. Mix using a hand-held blender until consistency becomes smooth.
3. Fold the whipped cream until fully incorporated into the cheese mixture.
4. Put mousse in 3 separate serving dishes topped with cinnamon.
5. Serve and enjoy immediately. If desired, cover and refrigerate first before serving.

Herbs & Goat Cheese Panna Cotta

Prep time: 20 min; **Cook time**: 10 min (requires refrigeration to set)

Serving Size: 1 glass; **Serves**: 6

Calories: 397; **Total Fat**: 38 g; **Protein**: 11 g;

Total Carbs: 3 g; **Net Carbs**: 3 g; **Sugar**: 2 g; **Fiber**: 0 g;

Ingredients

- ¾ cup of sour cream
- 1 ½ cups of heavy whipping cream
- 6 oz. goat cheese, soft
- 2 tsp. of unflavoured powdered gelatine
- 1 tsp. sea salt
- 1 tsp. of Herbes de Provence (available in most grocery stores)

Instructions

1. Combine the goat cheese, Herbes de Provence, heavy cream, and sour cream in a small-sized saucepan. Cook on medium heat setting. Stir constantly until the cheese melts.

2. Add salt and gelatine and whisk until everything is mixed completely.

3. Set heat to low and simmer for around 5 minutes while constantly stirring.

4. Pour the mixture into 6 small-sized glasses or ramekin evenly.

5. Refrigerate overnight or not less than 6 hours to set.

6. Serve in glasses. If preferred, dip glass in warm water first to loosen the panna cotta, and then invert the glass to transfer the contents to a small plate before serving.

7. Enjoy!

Coconut Blueberry Cream Bars

Prep time: 20 min;

Cook time: 5 min (requires refrigeration to set)

Serving Size: 1 bar; **Serves**: 20

Calories: 189; **Total Fat**: 20 g; **Protein**: 1 g;

Total Carbs: 3 g; **Net Carbs**: 3 g; **Sugar**: 3 g; **Fiber**: 0 g;

Ingredients

- 1 cup of fresh blueberries
- 8 oz. of butter
- ¾ cup of coconut oil
- 4 oz. of softened cream cheese, softened
- ¼ cup of coconut cream
- ¼ cup of granular Swerve

Instructions

1. Crush the blueberries gently in a small-sized bowl. Pour contents into an 8x8" glass or silicone baking dish.
2. Melt coconut oil and butter in a medium-sized saucepan over medium heat setting.
3. Take the dish away from heat. Allow to cook for around 5 minutes.
4. Put the remaining ingredients in the saucepan. Mix thoroughly using a wooden spoon.
5. Top the blueberries with the mixture. Put them in the freezer to set.
6. Take the saucepan out of the freezer and let it warm up a bit for around 15 minutes.
7. Cut the dish into 20 bars of equal size.
8. Serve and enjoy!

Panna Cotta Infused w/ Turmeric

Prep time: 20 min; **Cook time**: 8 min (requires refrigeration to set)

Serving Size: 1 glass; **Serves**: 6

Calories: 130; **Total Fat**: 12 g; **Protein**: 4 g;

Total Carbs: 3 g; **Net Carbs**: 3 g; **Sugar**: 0 g; **Fiber**: 0 g;

Ingredients

- 1 ½ cups of beef stock, homemade
- 1 ½ cups of coconut milk, refrigerated and water separated from cream
- 1 Tbsp. of turmeric
- ½ tbsp. of sea salt
- 1 ½ Tbsp. of unflavored powdered gelatin

Instructions

1. Heat the beef stock and coconut cream in a small-sized saucepan over medium heat setting.
2. Gradually whisk the gelatine in until it is completely incorporated.
3. Add some salt and turmeric, then allow to simmer for about 5 minutes.
4. Divide the mixture equally among 6 small-sized glasses or ramekins.
5. Refrigerate to set for 6 hours or overnight.
6. The dessert is best served and enjoyed cold.

Low-Fat Peach Cobblers (Sugar-Free)

Prep time: 5 min; **Cook time**: 15 min

Serving Size: 1 cup; **Serves**: 4

Calories: 80; **Total Fat**: 0.4 g; **Protein**: 6 g;

Total Carbs: 13.5 g; **Net Carbs**: 13 g; **Sugar**: 0 g; **Fiber**: 0.5 g;

Ingredients

- ¼ cup of Heart Smart Bisquick
- 1 large-sized egg
- ½ cup of skim milk
- 1 tsp. of Splenda
- 8 oz. of Del Monte Lite Peaches (diced and drained)

Instructions

1. Drain diced peaches and separate into 4 oven-safe, individual dessert cups.
2. Place Bisquick, egg, Splenda, and skim milk in a small-sized bowl, then mix well.
3. Pour ¼ of the mixture on top of each peach cup.
4. Bake for around 15 minutes at 400 degrees or until the topping turns brown.
5. Can be served hot or cold.

Cheesy Prosciutto Cup Muffin

Prep time: 20 min; **Cook time**: 12 min

Serving Size: 1 muffin; **Serves**: 1

Calories: 218; **Total Fat**: 15 g; **Protein**: 18 g;

Total Carbs: 2 g; **Net Carbs**: 2 g; **Sugar**: 0 g; **Fiber**: 0 g;

Ingredients

- 1 slice (1/2 oz.) of prosciutto
- 1 medium-sized egg yolk
- ½ oz. grated Parmesan cheese
- ½ oz. Brie cheese, diced
- 1/3 oz. mozzarella cheese, diced

Instructions

1. Set and pre-heat oven at 400° F.
2. Get a muffin tin that has around 1 ½" deep and 2 ½" wide hole.
3. Fold the prosciutto in half to make it squarish.
4. Put it in the muffin tin hole to completely line it.
5. Put the egg yolk in the prosciutto cup.
6. Gently top the egg yolk with the cheeses to avoid breaking the yolk.
7. Bake for approximately 12 minutes or until the yolk is warmed and cooked, but still runny.
8. Allow the muffin to cool for around 10 minutes before taking out of the muffin pan.
9. Serve and enjoy!

Chocolate Chia Pudding

Prep time: 20 min; Cook time: 0 min

Serving Size: 1 cup; **Serves**: 4

Calories: 277; **Total Fat**: 27 g; **Protein**: 3 g;

Total Carbs: 14 g; **Net Carbs**: 12 g; **Sugar**: 2 g; **Fiber**: 2 g;

Ingredients

- ¼ cup of chia seeds
- 1 cup of heavy cream
- 2 Tbsp. of granular Swerve or erythritol
- 2 Tbsp. of cocoa powder
- 1 Tbsp. of chocolate chips, sugar-free

Instructions

1. Set aside the chocolate chips, then mix the rest of the ingredients in a medium-sized bowl. Allow the mixture to sit for no less than 15 minutes, while stirring occasionally.
2. Divide equally among 4 cups.
3. Garnish each cup with the chocolate chips previously set aside.
4. Dessert is best enjoyed cold. It may be refrigerated for a maximum of 3 days.

Salty PB Cup Fudge

Prep time: 5 min; Cook time: 8 min

Serving Size: 1; Serves: 12

Calories: 150; **Total Fat**: 15 g; **Protein**: 3 g;

Total Carbs: 3 g; **Net Carbs**: 2 g; **Sugar**: 1 g; **Fiber**: 1 g;

Ingredients

- ½ cup of coconut oil
- ½ cup of almond butter
- 3 Tbsp. of cocoa powder
- 1 Tbsp. of vanilla extract
- 12 drops of liquid stevia
- 1 tsp. of coarse sea salt

Instructions

1. Heat a small-sized saucepan over medium setting. Melt the coconut oil and almond butter together.
2. Add the vanilla, cocoa powder, and stevia. Blend well by stirring.
3. Get a silicone candy mold and fill 12 slots with the mixture. Alternatively, you can use an ice cube tray with a silicone bottom.
4. Refrigerate to set for 2 hours or more.
5. Serve cold.

Conclusion

I hope this book was able to help you to not only understand the methods that make the ketogenic diet work, but also how to implement it in to your daily routine. I know that it can be quite daunting to make such a dramatic change to any part of your life, but when followed correctly, it won't take long for you to see the positive results of this eating plan!

The next step is to throw yourself in to your new way of living! Go through your kitchen and eliminate all of the non-ketogenic friendly foods. Make a list of ketogenic friendly ingredients and then get yourself to the grocery store to pick them up! You may find that it's easier to build your weekly menu before going to the grocery store. Doing this will help to ensure that you have food on hand at mealtime and prevent you from buying non-keto ingredients! After stocking up your kitchen, it just takes a little planning to set your new meal plan into action! Good luck!

Please Leave a Review!

If you like this book, I'd LOVE if you could leave a review.

It really would mean a lot to me.

Thanks :)

Raza Imam

Made in the USA
San Bernardino, CA
07 September 2018